Louisa May Alcott

Twayne's United States Authors Series

Lewis Leary, Editor
University of North Carolina, Chapel Hill

TUSAS 457

LOUISA MAY ALCOTT
(1832–1888)
Photograph courtesy of
Concord Free Public Library

Louisa May Alcott

By Ruth K. MacDonald

Northeastern University

Twayne Publishers • *Boston*

Louisa May Alcott

Ruth K. MacDonald

Copyright © 1983 by G. K. Hall & Company
All Rights Reserved
Published by Twayne Publishers
A Division of G. K. Hall & Company
70 Lincoln Street
Boston, Massachusetts 02111

Book Production by Marne B. Sultz

Book Design by Barbara Anderson

Printed on permanent/durable acid-free
paper and bound in the United States of
America.

Library of Congress Cataloging in Publication Data

MacDonald, Ruth K.
Louisa May Alcott.

(Twayne's United States authors series; TUSAS
457)
Bibliography: p. 103
Includes index.
1. Alcott, Louisa May, 1832–1888—
Criticism and interpretation.
I. Title.   II. Series.
PS1018.M28   1983   813'.4   83-12675
ISBN 0-8057-7397-5

For Eva Reynolds Cook and Jessie MacLeod MacDonald

Contents

About the Author

Ruth K. MacDonald is an assistant professor of English at Northeastern University in Boston, where she teaches literature for children. She received her B.A. and M.A. from the University of Connecticut and a Ph.D. from Rutgers University. She is president of the Children's Literature Association and has chaired the division of children's literature for the Modern Language Association and the section on children's literature for the Northeast Modern Language Association. Her book *Literature for Children in England and America, 1646–1774* (Troy, NY: Whitston Press, 1982) is a study of the various genres of literature for children in the period. She has published a number of articles in various periodicals and dictionaries on both British and American children's literature in the eighteenth and nineteenth centuries. She has been a guest lecturer on literature for children at the University of California at Los Angeles; Wheaton College, Norton, Massachusetts; and Middlesex County College, Edison, New Jersey.

Preface

Louisa May Alcott has received a great deal of critical attention in recent years for a number of different reasons: the discovery and publication of her "thrillers," the gothic short stories which are unlike any of the works she ever wrote for children; a renewed interest in her adult works in general, especially her novels *Moods* and *Work;* a new interest in children's literature by critics of adult literature; and feminist critics' reexamination of women's works frequently not included in the canon of traditional literature. That Alcott should be the focus of so much attention is a tribute to her versatility as a writer and to the enduring quality of her works.

Much attention, however, has been superficial. Alcott biographers have not always evaluated her works critically and objectively. Anyone who wishes to study this eminent author owes a debt to Madeleine B. Stern's *Louisa May Alcott* (Norman: University of Oklahoma, 1950), as well as to Martha Saxton's *Louisa May; A Modern Biography of Louisa May Alcott* (Boston: Houghton Mifflin, 1977). But Stern's biography hardly touches the surface of her literary productions, and Saxton's is unsympathetic to her works for children. This latter book seeks to examine in close detail both the novels for children, which have been glossed over in laudatory reviews for the last century, and the novels for adults which have only recently been discovered. But Saxton finds little to praise in Alcott's works for children. In both areas of Alcott's writing I have sought by close reading to examine the complexity that Alcott at her best included in her characterization and plotting; it is a temptation for any of her readers simply to see the connections between her experiences, frequently her source of inspiration, and her writing itself, and to conclude that she was simply autobiographical. The loving, optimistic, simple exterior that her children's books present is frequently judged to be the quality of the author's life and her vision of it. But an examination of her adult works, which show a sensibility far more complex and troubled, and a further examination of her children's works, especially as they refer to events in her own life as she fictionalized them for public consumption, reveal a richer understanding of life than has been heretofore acknowledged. Her adult works show an understanding of the more troubled aspects of her own personality, and her children's books show the sometimes uneasy but frequently compelling and unavoidable ways in which she resolved them for her public and for herself.

I have also attempted to place Alcott's works for children within the context of her works for both children and adults, and in the broader context of literature for children in America at the time. Alcott wrote for children during the flourishing and flowering of such literature; her contemporaries were Mary Mapes Dodge, author of *Hans Brinker; or the Silver Skates,* and editor of *St. Nicholas* magazine for children; Mark Twain, whose *Prince and the Pauper* was serialized in *St. Nicholas;* Susan Coolidge and Martha Finley Farquharson, to name just a few of the American authors for children. As for British writers, Lewis Carroll's *Alice in Wonderland* preceded *Little Women* by only three years. Alcott was aware of these other writers and what they wrote; though she sometimes pretended not to be very interested in her works for children, saying that she preferred to write for adults, she nevertheless engaged in the lively discussion concerning the quality and nature of literature for children which went on during the period of incredible proliferation of works for children. In a number of ways Alcott was a setter of trends, not only in her pronouncements on works for children, but also in her works themselves; their uniqueness among her contemporaries is a primary focus here.

At the same time, Alcott knew and read the authors of adult literature of her time and was personally acquainted with a number of them. It is impossible to deal with her writing thoroughly and to ignore her indebtedness to her numerous literary connections; nor have I tried to do so. The examinations here include her adult novels and gothic short stories.

With one particular novel, *Moods,* her first adult and favorite novel, I have examined an issue that has not been commented on at all by other critics—the difference between the 1864 version and the 1881 reissue, where Alcott reinserted much that had been cut from the earlier edition and rewrote the story considerably. The contrast between the two reveals Alcott's original intention in the book as well as her more mature reconsideration of its themes. Furthermore, there is virtually no comment on Alcott's gothic novel *A Modern Mephistophiles;* here I have paid special attention to the similarities between Alcott's book and Goethe's *Faust,* an obvious source of her inspiration. The closer focus on the adult works is an attempt to fill the void in critical attention to Alcott's adult novels. Though Alcott was prolific as a short story writer, these stories usually have not endured nor are they an important part of the Alcott canon. I have referred to them only as they are connected with her novels.

Finally, an assessment of the long-lasting vitality of Alcott's best works for children is particularly important. Though her works for adults shed new light on her career and give the reader a glimpse of a side of her literary life frequently missed by the average reader of her children's works (that reader who is most likely to be a child and not a scholar at all), these adult works have long since passed out of the reading of anyone but scholars and historians of literature. But *Little Women* and her other books for children have endured, especially among girls and the women they grow up to be. Yet it is not simply nostalgia and sentimentality that keep *Little Women* on the shelves of libraries and bookstores; there is a complex relationship between reader and message, and its complexities keep readers of all ages loyal. The book sometimes represents different experiences for child and adult readers, and its richness and depth are worth the examination of students and scholars of literature for any age of reader.

Ruth K. MacDonald

Northeastern University

Chronology

1830   Amos Bronson Alcott and Abba May married in Boston, Massachusetts, May 23.

1831   Move to Germantown, Pennsylvania; Anna Bronson Alcott born March 16.

1832   Louisa May Alcott born in Germantown, November 29.

1834   Alcotts move to Boston. Bronson organizes Temple School, September 22.

1835   Elizabeth Peabody Alcott (later Elizabeth Sewall Alcott) born June 24.

1840   Temple School fails. Family moves to Concord, March 31. Abigail May Alcott born July 16.

1842   Bronson Alcott goes to England, May 8; returns October 20 with Charles Lane and makes plans to form a utopian community.

1843   Alcotts and Lane move to Fruitlands, Harvard, Massachusetts, June 1.

1844   Fruitlands experiment fails; Alcotts move to Still River, Harvard, January 16; return to Concord, November 14.

1845   Alcotts move into Hillside house, Concord, now called Wayside.

1848   Family returns to Boston. Abba Alcott establishes social agency to help the poor.

1851   Louisa May Alcott's first poem, "Sunlight," appears in *Peterson's Magazine* in September.

1852   First story, "The Rival Painters," published in *Olive Branch,* May 8; during December hears Theodore Parker's sermons at Music Hall, Boston.

1854   *Flower Fables.*

1856   Family contracts scarlet fever in May; all recover.

1858   Family moves to Orchard House, Concord; Elizabeth Alcott dies, March 14; Anna Alcott announces engagement to John Bridge Pratt, April 7.

1860   Boston Theatre Company produces Alcott's *Nat Bachelor's Pleasure Trip,* May 4; Anna Alcott and John Pratt married, May 23.

1862   Louisa Alcott goes to Washington, D.C., as Civil War nurse, December 14.

1863   First gothic short story, "Pauline's Passion and Punishment," in *Frank Leslie's Illustrated Newspaper,* January 3, 10. Returns to Concord to recuperate from typhoid, January 22. "Hospital Sketches" published in *Commonwealth Magazine,* May 22–June 26. James Redpath publishes collected *Hospital Sketches.*

1864   *Moods.*

1865   Alcott leaves for Europe, July 20.

1866   Returns to Concord, July 22.

1868   Assumes editorship of *Merry's Museum,* January; January issue contains Christmas Breakfast scene from *Little Women. Little Women* published in September.

1869   *Good Wives.*

1870   *An Old-Fashioned Girl;* Alcott goes to Europe with sister May and Alice Bartlett, April 1; John Pratt dies, November 28; Alcott begins *Little Men.*

1871   *Little Men;* Alcott returns to Boston, June 6.

1873   *Work* serialized in *Christian Union* beginning December 18, concurrently published in book form by Roberts Brothers.

1875   *Eight Cousins;* October, attends Women's Congress in Syracuse, New York; November, goes to New York City, spends Christmas holidays there.

1876   *Rose in Bloom;* leads counterdemonstration by local women at the Concord celebration of the Centennial, July 4.

1877   *A Modern Mephistophiles;* Alcott moves to Thoreau House, Concord Village, November 14; Abba Alcott dies, November 25.

1878   *Under the Lilacs.* May Alcott marries Ernest Nieriker in Paris, March 22.

1879   Alcott first woman to register to vote in Concord; Louisa May Nieriker born in Paris, November 8; May Alcott Nieriker dies in Paris, December 29, leaving daughter to the care of Louisa May Alcott.

1881   *Jack and Jill;* Louisa Nieriker arrives in Boston, fall; *Moods* revised and reissued by Roberts Brothers.

1884   Louisa and Bronson Alcott increasingly unwell; family moves to Boston to be near doctors.

1886   *Jo's Boys.*

1887   Louisa Alcott adopts nephew John Sewell Pratt (afterwards John S. P. Alcott) to provide heir to her royalties and make legal arrangements for her family in case of her death.

1888   Amos Bronson Alcott dies, March 4; Louisa May Alcott dies, March 6; both buried in Sleepy Hollow Cemetery, Concord, following joint funeral.

1893   Anna Alcott Pratt edits and publishes Louisa Alcott's *Comic Tragedies.*

Chapter One

The Realist of Concord

Whenever one studies a writer, it is generally necessary to know something of his or her life and times. In the case of Louisa May Alcott, this information is particularly important, since Alcott's personal experiences influenced her writing more than is typical of most other writers. Her family provided her with the subject of her best-known book, and even when she was inventing material, real-life situations provided the actual events. Though she was surrounded most of her life by the leading transcendentalists, and though she was impressed and influenced by their ideas, she was herself a realist of the first order. In her writing and her life she dealt with reality, analyzing and attempting to understand it, rather than emphasizing abstract ideas and literary trends.

It is a surprise to find out that the woman whose life and work was intimately connected with Boston and its environs, especially Concord, Massachusetts, was born in Germantown, Pennsylvania. Her father, the transcendentalist and educator Bronson Alcott, was director of a school for small children there, sponsored by a wealthy Quaker businessman. Her mother, Abba May Alcott, was a member of one of the leading families in Boston, related by marriage to John Hancock. Louisa May Alcott was born on November 29, 1832, her father's thirty-third birthday. In temperament and appearance she was like her mother's family—energetic, temperamental, tall, and dark—rather than her fair and placid father, whom her older sister Anna and younger sisters Elizabeth and May resembled. All four of the girls were subjects of their father's educational scrutiny, for he began at their births to keep records of their behavior, especially when they were disciplined or taught, in order to understand how the human mind works. His diary about the girls stands as one of the first attempts in child psychology to record the behaviors of children.

Bronson Alcott's educational methods were unconventional for his time, and when his wealthy patron died, he brought his family back to Boston. There he founded the Temple School, named after the Masonic Temple in which it stood, with the help of Elizabeth Palmer Peabody, afterwards acknowledged as the founder of the modern kindergarten. Bronson Alcott's teaching methods came into conflict with nineteenth-century mores; though the school lasted for six years, when he began to discuss childbirth with his pupils and admitted a black student to the school, the force of public opinion and the decreasing number of students forced him to close, leaving him in deep debt for the furnishings of the school and the family's lodgings.

This was the last time during his daughters' childhoods that Bronson Alcott had regular employment and a steady income. Until Louisa Alcott established her reputation as a children's writer with the financial and critical success of *Little Women,* the family was constantly in debt and always moving, financially dependent on whatever small contributions the female members of the family could make, and on donations from friends and relatives. After the Temple School closed, Bronson decided that Boston was simply not prepared to accept him and his advanced ideas. He moved his family to Concord to be near his new friends, Ralph Waldo Emerson and Henry David Thoreau. The Alcotts lived in what is now called Wayside, a house later inhabited by the Nathaniel Hawthornes and even later by Margaret Sidney, author of *The Five Little Peppers* (1880). It is less than a mile from the Emerson house and an easy walk to Walden Pond.

Of all the people Bronson Alcott ever knew, he was closest to Emerson. Though he was friendly with Thoreau and let him teach his daughters botany while tramping through the woods, he remained a lifelong intimate of Emerson, and not simply because Emerson would lend him considerable sums of money. Louisa Alcott also knew and admired both Emerson and Thoreau; in her adolescence and young womanhood they were both sources of romantic fantasies for her. She memorialized Emerson as the kind and beneficent Mr. Laurence in *Little Women.* Thoreau became the model for the romantic interests in her adult novels and for the wild boys in her juvenile novels, such as Dan Kean of *Little Men* and *Jo's Boys.*

In 1842 Bronson Alcott traveled to Europe, financed by Emerson, to meet other educational theorists and to exchange ideas. He arrived home the following autumn with Charles Lane, with whom he had decided to found a utopian community. On June 1, 1843, the whole Alcott family, Charles Lane and his son, and several followers moved to Harvard, Massachusetts, where they all became "the consociate family," based on the principles of vegetarianism and communal work and learning.

Though the Fruitlands community, as it was called, lasted for less than eight months, disbanding in January of the following year, the experience had a profound effect on the Alcott family and especially on Louisa.

During his association with Lane, Bronson Alcott contemplated leaving his family and joining the Shaker community in upper New York State with Lane. Bronson called his family together to discuss the possibility of his leaving, but made no move. After the demise of the community, Bronson suffered a nervous breakdown, and though he recovered, he was never again the leader of the family. Instead, the Alcotts were ruled by Abba Alcott, and supported by her labor and that of her daughters, especially Louisa.

From the time of the Fruitlands experiment it was clear to the young Louisa that her father was not a reliable supporter of his family, either financially or emotionally. The family members certainly knew that Bronson's labors would never earn enough to support the family of six. But the fact that he was willing to abandon them, albeit for philosophical motives and with their discussion of the matter, combined with his unresponsive, almost comatose presence after the nervous breakdown, served only to underscore the man's distance from and irresponsibility about his dependents. It became clear to Louisa that her mother relied on her not only for the emotional support that a wife might otherwise have expected from her husband, but also, as Louisa became older, for financial support.

From this point on, Louisa would live and work for her family. Nearly all the proceeds from her writing would go for their maintenance. She even chose to forego the fulfillment and security of marriage so that the Alcott family might have her undivided attention. She maintained this posture of self-sacrifice until the end of her life, much longer, in fact, than necessary, for the family members had found other people to depend on and the earlier proceeds from Louisa's books had made them financially secure. Self-abnegation simply became a habit.

After the Fruitlands experience, the Alcotts rented rooms in Still River, Massachusetts, and then in Concord. It became apparent that a family without inheritance could not long live without at least one of its members earning a steady income, so when Mrs. Alcott was offered the opportunity to become a social worker in Boston, she moved her family back to the city to be near her work. The Alcott bias about blacks and German immigrants became apparent at this time, for Mrs. Alcott proclaimed in various reports to her patrons that the Irish to whom she ministered were shiftless, lazy, and dirty. When she later started an intelligence office to match women willing to work as domestic servants with women who required such help, she railed against the destitute Irish whom she claimed were unwilling to help themselves.

This bias is evident in Louisa Alcott's adult novel *Work*, where the heroine, Christie Devon, consents to work as a parlormaid alongside a black cook, but will not work with an Irish girl. Christie's experiences as a domestic servant were drawn largely from Alcott's own experiences at the time her mother suggested she take on a maid's job when one turned up at the intelligence office and there was no one else to fill it. Though the Alcotts were a remarkably open-minded family, supporting abolition, women's rights, and philanthropy, especially for working women, their one blind spot was the Irish, an oversight that Louisa inherited and expressed in her novels without even examining the real or imagined source of her prejudice.

It was during this period in Boston that Elizabeth Alcott, the model for Beth March in *Little Women,* contracted scarlet fever from an immigrant family, a charity case of Mrs. Alcott's. Elizabeth had always been a quiet girl, too nervous to go to school, staying home to care for her family since she had no outside life of her own. She never recovered from the disease, but gradually weakened from complications of the high fever and died in December, 1857. The family had tried to revive her spirits by moving to Walpole, New Hampshire, in 1855, but the move had little effect.

After the family moved to New Hampshire, Louisa Alcott established a pattern of living alternately in Boston for a few months in order to write and to work at odd sewing and teaching jobs, and returning to live with her family. She began to publish short stories of a sentimental kind in the *Boston Evening Gazette* in 1855 and later in the *Atlantic Monthly,* and she may have tried acting for a brief time with the Boston Theatre Company. Her farce, *Nat Bachelor's Pleasure Trip,* was presented at the Howard Atheneum on May 4, 1860.

In December, 1854, George Briggs published Alcott's first work for children, *Flower Fables,* a collection of fairy stories that she had written for Emerson's daughter, Ellen, when Alcott had been her teacher in Concord. Though Boston offered Alcott the freedom to enjoy herself and the privacy to write, demands at home frequently called her back to attend to some emergency or to nurse a family member through an illness.

When the family moved into the only permanent home they ever really had in Concord, the Orchard House, down the road from their earlier home at Wayside, Alcott continued this pattern of alternating family duties in Concord and writing in Boston. With the death of Elizabeth and the marriage of her sister Anna to John Pratt in May, 1860, the family was considerably smaller, so that Alcott could have her own room in the house for her writing, a convenient arrangement as long as no one interrupted her.

Alcott mourned the breaking up of her family; she likened her sister's marriage to a second funeral, and felt betrayed that her sister had found someone to depend on and to confide in, intimacies which she had formerly shared with Louisa. As the Civil War commenced, Louisa Alcott cast about for a purpose in her life, one which would absorb the energy that had formerly gone into her care for her family and her writing, which she felt was progressing too slowly to satisfy her. She had just turned thirty years old, the age at which a Victorian woman officially became a spinster.

The war presented her with just such a cause. While she stayed home, sewing and scraping lint as her contribution to the Union effort, she turned her mind to the more active career of nursing. In December, 1862, she went to Washington, D.C., as a hospital nurse, one of Dorothea Dix's nurses in the U.S. Sanitary Commission. She was assigned to the Union Hotel Hospital, a hastily converted building with poor ventilation, insufficient light, stale water, inadequate facilities for any kind of hygiene, and doctors who practiced the kind of medicine that is now known to cause more harm than good. To any Victorian woman the sight of wounded men would have been shocking; the duty of undressing and scrubbing new casualties so that the extent of their injuries could be determined would have frightened other women to the extent that they would have fled back to the comfort of their homes. The diet of tea, potatoes, and rancid beef might very well have been indigestible to a vegetarian born and raised as Alcott was. The long hours of nursing necessitated by the huge number of wounded arriving from the disastrous rout of the Union forces at the battle of Fredericksburg, combined with the bad diet, bad air, and the shock of such intimate contact with men undoubtedly weakened Alcott's resistance to disease. After six weeks of nursing, she was sent home with typhoid fever.

Although her nursing experience was a short one, it changed Alcott's life. She was never well again, primarily because of the debilitating effects of mercury poisoning from the calomel treatment taken to cure the typhoid. Her bones ached and her hair fell out. For an active woman like Alcott, the confinement of an invalid was even more difficult to bear. But even more important to the course of her life, while convalescing, Alcott reworked for publication the letters she had written to her family from Washington. *Hospital Sketches* (1863) established her reputation as a serious author. The book was popular in the North not only because it was obviously written by a Union partisan, but also because it showed a lively sense of detail and frankness. At this time Alcott was also writing her "potboilers," anonymous and pseudonymous gothic thrillers which made money but not reputation. Though she continued to write the thrillers,

Alcott turned her hand more seriously to high literature after the publication of *Hospital Sketches*. The result was her first novel, *Moods* (1864), which was not well received because of the improbability of the characters and events.

In 1865 Alcott toured Europe as a companion to an invalid girl. Although it was always her fervent wish to tour the Continent, the increasing demands and the passivity of her traveling companion made the trip something of a trial. But she visited Germany, Switzerland, France, and England, meeting Ladislas Wisniewski, a young Polish revolutionary whose high spirits were the models for Laurie's pranks in *Little Women*. When she returned to Boston a year later, she found her family in debt and unable to manage their affairs without her.

Once again she turned her hand toward the support of her family, composing thrillers and publishing stories in a children's magazine, *Merry's Museum,* as a contributing editor. When she became the magazine's official editor in 1867, Thomas Niles, an editor at the Roberts Brothers publishing house, suggested she write a novel for girls. Alcott balked, since she claimed to know nothing about girls; but using the events of her sisters' lives as inspiration, she produced the first half of what is now known as *Little Women*. Encouraged by the sales following the book's publication on September 30, 1868, she moved to Boston on November first and wrote a chapter a day, completing the second half of the book on January 1, 1869. The effort brought on her recurring illness, and in the spring Alcott took a vacation to Canada and Maine. She returned in August, a famous and well-to-do woman.

She continued her success as a children's writer by producing *An Old-Fashioned Girl* in 1870. In 1871, while she was again touring Europe, she heard of the death of her brother-in-law John Pratt and decided to write *Little Men* as a tribute to him and as a financial support for her sister and two nephews, even though Pratt had already made adequate arrangements. She returned from Europe with a collection of short stories which she published as *Shawl-Straps,* one of the volumes in her collection of short stories called *Aunt Jo's Scrapbag.* The series continued throughout the rest of her life using stories she had published in various magazines which were then collected and republished in order to turn a double profit.

In 1873, when Henry Ward Beecher approached Alcott about writing an adult novel to be serialized in his magazine *The Christian Union,* she returned to an autobiographical novel that she had begun in 1860, then called *Success.* She quickly rewrote it, retitling it *Work: A Story of Experience.* Beecher published it serially in 1873; Roberts Brothers, her publisher, brought the book out as a whole also in 1873. Christie Devon, the heroine of the novel, is as much an autobiographical creation as was Jo March. In the novel Alcott points out the difficulties that an energetic, educated young woman had in earning a respectable living for herself, and espoused honest, hard work as fulfilling and redemptive.

Back in Boston in 1874, Alcott and her father attended the debates at the State House on woman suffrage. When she went on vacation to Conway, New Hampshire, that summer, Alcott wrote the first of two books about girls' education and manners, *Eight Cousins.* She obviously had the second novel, *Rose in Bloom,* in mind when she promised it to her public in the preface to *Eight Cousins,* but in between the writing of the two she spent a winter on vacation, attending the Women's Congress of 1875 in Syracuse, playing the celebrated authoress at Vassar College, and spending her Christmas in New York City, visiting at the Tombs, the Newsboys Lodging House, and the Randall's Island orphanage. Many of the opinions she heard voiced in Syracuse and many of her experiences with the poor in New York City appeared in *Rose in Bloom.* Her thoughts about the rights of women and girls were made public in the *Woman's Journal,* founded in Boston in 1870 by Lucy Stone and Henry Blackwell. When women were excluded from the Centennial festivities in Concord in 1876, she reported their counterdemonstration for the *Woman's Journal;* she also recorded her own registration as a voter in Concord, in 1879.

Alcott's mother, now in failing health, wished to return to Concord, so the family moved back to Orchard House in early 1876, where Alcott wrote *Rose in Bloom.* In 1877 her publisher asked her to contribute a novel to the No Name series of books by well-known authors of the time who would nevertheless compose the works in the series anonymously. Alcott reworked a novella which she had submitted as one of her longer thrillers in 1866 but which had been rejected as too sensational. Influenced by her recent reading of Goethe's *Faust,* she rewrote and submitted *A Modern Mephistophiles* in her earlier lurid style which was quite unlike her works for children. While she nursed her mother through her final illness, she wrote *Under the Lilacs,* which was serialized in Mary Mapes Dodge's *St. Nicholas* magazine, a new monthly publication for children. She also supervised the purchase of the Thoreau house in Concord village, to which the family moved only days before her mother's death. Abba May Alcott died on November 25, 1877.

After her mother's death, Alcott and her father were drawn closer than· ever before in mutual understanding and in recognition of their temperamental differences and yet of their common bond as Alcotts. Living in

Concord village and visiting with the neighboring children gave Alcott the inspiration for a new book for Mrs. Dodge, *Jack and Jill* (1880). A. K. Loring's return of the copyright of *Moods*, her first and favorite novel, suggested to Alcott the possibility that she might rewrite it, restoring many of the descriptive passages that Loring had advised her to cut out and eliminating the elegant language that she had affected in her youth. Roberts Brothers was happy to republish the long-ignored work of their most famous author, this time under her copyright, in 1881.

Both Alcott and her father became increasingly ill with age, Bronson suffering a stroke in 1882, and both turned to such cures as homeopathy, Christian Science, and hypnotism when traditional medicine failed them. Alcott's sister May had married a Swiss banker in 1878 and had invited Alcott to visit them in France, where they had settled. She was never able to make the trip, though she thought at length about the differences between the two sisters' lives, beginning a so-called art story about them, *Diana and Perses,* which she never finished but which has recently been discovered and published. When May died in December, 1880, after the birth of her first child, she asked that her sister assume the care of Louisa's namesake, Louisa May Nieriker.

With the arrival of little Lulu, as the child was called, Orchard House became quite crowded, since Alcott's only remaining sister Anna and her two sons frequently stayed there with the rest of the family. In 1884 Orchard House was sold and the whole family moved to Boston to larger quarters in a rented house in Louisburg Square. Though Alcott was old to be a new mother, being forty-eight years old when Lulu arrived, she did as well as she could, writing the stories that appeared in the *Lulu's Library* series for the little girl, and hiring a nanny to help when she was too unwell. She often stayed at the rest home of a woman doctor, Rhoda Lawrence (one of the first women graduates of the Boston medical schools), who became her close friend and the inspiration for Dr. Nan of *Jo's Boys* (1886). The public had long clamored for another book about the March family, and Alcott complied, although her ill health and the pain she felt in dealing with the characters of Marmee and Amy, who represented her dead mother and sister, made the writing difficult. The book is full of the sadness in which it was written, and Alcott made sure that no one asked for another sequel by carefully tying up all the loose ends, marrying off or killing her characters, as seemed appropriate, in a grand finale. It was to be her last novel.

Alcott kept writing until the time of her death, planning a new collection of short stories for adolescent girls, published posthumously as

A Garland for Girls. She also consented to reissue *A Modern Mephistophiles,* this time with her name on it, also printed after her death. But Alcott sensed that she had not long to live early in 1887. When she visited her father on March 4, she realized that he too was dying. Bronson died that night. When the mourners arrived to pay their respects, they were told that Louisa had died in her sleep at Dr. Lawrence's rest home early on the morning of March 6. Father and daughter were eulogized at a joint funeral and were buried in the Alcott family plot in Sleepy Hollow Cemetery, Concord, next to the graves of Abba and Elizabeth Alcott.

Chapter Two
The March Family Stories

The March family stories, *Little Women, Good Wives, Little Men,* and *Jo's Boys,* are the best-known and best-written of Alcott's juvenile novels. After her initial success with *Little Women,* her public was willing and even demanding to read almost anything else she wrote—short stories, novels about other families, even reissues of adult novels. Alcott was continually under pressure to produce more stories for children, both from her publisher and from readers. But while they would read almost anything she wrote with approval, her readers were particularly insistent about their desire for more works about Alcott's interesting family, the Marches. The meteoric success of *Little Women* encouraged her to write its sequel, *Good Wives,* almost immediately after the first book's publication in 1868. Though she satisfied her hungry public with other works for a few years, in 1871 she wrote *Little Men,* and again, for a few years at least, the public was satisfied. It was not until 1880 that Alcott again picked up the story of the Marches; in the intervening years her public had not stopped demanding more of the stories, but Alcott had been ill for some time, and at other times busy with other projects and stories. Beyond her other diversions, the last March story was hard to approach because of the pain it caused her to write about her family; her home life had never been easy, and many of the people who were the original models for characters had died. That it took her six years to finish *Jo's Boys* is more than an indication of her weariness and declining health at the end of her life; it also shows how difficult the writing was.

The usual critical comment about the March works deals with the autobiographical component in them; it is true that some of the characters were inspired by people Alcott knew, and that many of the incidents were taken from her own experiences. But even in the first book of the series and the most autobiographical of the group, *Little Women,* Alcott was not simply being reportorial about the lives of her sisters and parents. The Alcott family story underwent considerable revision before it was acceptably fictionalized into the March family story for adolescent girls. The Alcott family, although tightly knit, was never as normal or as free of hostility as the March family is; a lifetime of living with the various quirks and failings of her otherwise exceptional parents and siblings had left Alcott with many ill feelings which could not be aired in as public a statement as a book. The closeness of the March family, as well as the various characters' sincerity and warmth, are a result of Alcott's ability to make autobiography into consistent, convincing fiction, even though the result was sometimes the pretty, somewhat sentimental pictures of a family life that never was.

After the first story Alcott fictionalized to an even greater extent. Her public demanded to see the March sisters married off, then to see their offspring, and finally to see how these children married. Alcott invented spouses and children in abundance, as well as worthy professions and vocations for the children to grow into. These spouses, children, and vocations may never have existed in real life, and if they did, Alcott sometimes revised them considerably to make the fiction more consistent and plausible. The Alcotts and their friends were, after all, an unconventional bunch, and their lives were sometimes so unusual that her reading public would hardly have accepted their fates were they simply transcribed unchanged in her novels. Some of the characters are so conventional in Alcott's reworking of them that modern scholars have criticized her for bowing excessively low to the demands of her public; many feel that she should have stayed closer to real life, and that giving in to the public as she did was an artistic compromise. Such it may have been, but Alcott could not entirely disregard her public, nor could she break with impunity the conventions of the domestic novels for girls without losing her readers. To try the artistically adventurous would have been too dangerous, especially given that her writing was to support her family. In the end, some compromise was necessary to keep the profits coming in.

But there are signs of the artistic tension that Alcott maintained in order not to bend utterly to public demand, small clues that have been overlooked by critics, indicating a certain subversive strain in Alcott's compliance with the demands of the children's novel. This is more the case with the March family stories than with any of the other juvenile novels that she wrote. And even in following the conventions of the children's novel, Alcott broke much new ground for her time. These novels are unique among her contemporaries for their fully rounded characterization, including the characters' faults and struggles as well as their virtues, for the restraint in the preachiness which overwhelmed works of many of her contemporaries, for the simple but accurate style with which she portrayed the warmth of family life, and for her skill as a local colorist of nineteenth-century New England.

Little Women

Louisa May Alcott wrote *Little Women* in 1868, when she was thirty-five years old. She was already a writer of some repute; she had published a collection of fairy tales for children, *Flower Fables,* in 1854. She had written many short stories, both sentimental and gothic, for various periodicals. A collection of her letters to her family from her post in Washington, D.C., as a Civil War nurse had been published in 1863; *Hospital Sketches* established her reputation as adult writer. She even published a novel for adults entitled *Moods* (1864). She was also editor of *Merry's Museum,* a monthly periodical for children. *Little Women* was, therefore, not the work of a beginner, but rather that of a seasoned writer, skilled in a number of different genres. But it was not until the publication of *Little Women* that Alcott gained the reputation that she holds today as an outstanding writer of children's books. In fact, had she not written *Little Women,* even with her adult books and her seven other juvenile books, her name would probably be an obscure footnote in the history of American writers.

The idea of writing a girl's book did not originate with Alcott herself. Thomas Niles of Roberts Brothers Publishing Company in Boston urged her to try her hand at the génre, to compete with the "Oliver Optic" books of William T. Adams, published by a rival Boston publishing company, Lee and Shepard.[1] Alcott had her doubts about her ability to write for girls, but as she cast about for her plot and characters, she settled on the girls she knew best, her sisters and herself, and their lives as they were growing up in Concord. She had already written a short story modeled at least partly on their lives in "The Sisters' Trial" for the *Saturday Evening Gazette* (January 26, 1856, quarto series, no. 4). Her elder sister's court-ship had been the inspiration for "A Modern Cinderella" for the *Atlantic Monthly* (October, 1860, vol. 6, no. 36). Her family life had already proved its availability and appropriateness for short story material, so she turned her hand to making her sisters' lives into a novel for girls.

She apparently had the idea for the book in January, 1868, while she was busy editing *Merry's Museum,* for in the first number that she edited appeared one of the earliest incidents of the book, the sisters' sacrifice of their Christmas breakfast. The incident is more autobiographical in

Merry's Museum; the sisters have the names they did in real life: Nan, Lu, Beth, and May. In addition, Alcott uses first-person narration, her own character saying about the tasty breakfast, "I wish we'd eaten it up," a feeling shared by many readers. Here was the material for a book already at hand; the task remained merely to turn autobiography into fiction.

The book nearly wrote itself. While Alcott did not find herself in the "vortex" of scribbling fever that characterized her earlier writing attempts, she wrote steadily and regularly with hardly any revisions. It took about six weeks to write the 402 pages of the first half. She turned the manuscript over to Mr. Niles on July 15, 1868; on September 30 it was published.

The story is based roughly on the lives of the four teen-aged Alcott sisters and their mother during their years at Hillside house in Concord. The plot is episodic in structure, with individual chapters devoted to an individual sister; however, the unifying theme is the quest of each sister to overcome her "burden" in life and become a "little woman."

Jo is the second eldest at fifteen, and the most interesting character in the book. She is the character modeled after Alcott herself. She is a writer of plays, poems, and short stories, an adventurous and spirited girl whose burden is her boyish nature underneath her girlish form. In the course of the book she reconciles herself to being a girl and learns the domesticity, poise, and grace that qualify her as a "little woman" at the book's close. She also learns to control a violent temper. Meg is the eldest, sixteen at the beginning of the book. Her besetting sin is vanity; she likes fine clothing and fancy balls, but as a poor girl, she must learn to devote herself to her family and not to wish for expensive finery and luxuries. Beth, aged thirteen, is a shy, housewifely little girl whose faults are small; she learns to overcome her shyness and her occasional desire to turn away from her domestic duties to have fun. Indeed, her burden is so light that she is almost the perfect "little woman" at the beginning of the book. Amy is the youngest sister, ten years old, and spoiled and indulged because of her age. She has artistic talent, but her plans are sometimes so grandiose as to be impractical. She must overcome the thoughtlessness that comes with being so indulged and must learn to help others.

The next-door neighbors, Mr. Laurence and his grandson Theodore Laurence, or Laurie, provide much of the fun and excitement in the story. Mr. Laurence gives the girls a Christmas party, Beth a piano, and Jo the freedom of his library. He also lends the Marches his grandson Laurie, who is Jo's age and just as adventurous and wild as she is. He is a rich orphan, interested in music, who grinds away at his studies and then slips away to the Marches for various romps with the girls. As the story progresses, he proposes to Jo, is refused, and eventually marries Amy.

Though Jo may be the most interesting character, the most central and important to the book's theme and progress is Marmee, the mother of the March sisters. She is the center of the household, the guide for the girls when they are confused, their confessor when they have done wrong, their confidante when they are troubled. She is always there when she is needed, always strong and loving, always knowing what to do. She seems at first too good to be true, for she is the ideal mother that any reader would want. But she is also quite human, with a temper which she can control, but cannot conquer, and with the doubts and fears for her daughters that any loving mother has.

Good Wives.   *Little Women* was an overnight success, not just with girls but with the reading public in general. In it Alcott relied exclusively on her family history, making whatever changes were necessary to transform autobiography into fiction and thus bringing the story up to Meg's engagement to John Brooke. Her audience reacted to the book by requesting a second half, showing how the March sisters married. For this sequel, commencing with Meg's wedding day and ending with Jo's marriage to Professor Bhaer, which is now published with the first part, Alcott turned almost exclusively to fiction. However, her sister Anna, the Meg of the novel, had married; she had two sons: not the twins Daisy and Demi of *Good Wives.* Her sister Lizzie, the Beth of *Little Women,* had died, so that inventing a partner for her was not necessary. But both Alcott and her sister May, Jo and Amy in the story, were unmarried, so that if Alcott were to do as her readers decreed and marry them off, appropriate spouses would have to be fabricated. The biggest fabrication of them all, Laurie, who was no particular boy, but rather an amalgam of several young men whom Alcott knew throughout her life, had to be dealt with, and carefully, too. He is the most eligible bachelor in the book—young, handsome, mannerly, entertaining, and rich, a good catch for any girl in the neighborhood.[2] By the end of the second part of the book he has been rejected by Jo and has turned to Amy. Together the two make a conventional romantic couple.

For Jo, Alcott invents Professor Bhaer; the two marry and found the Plumfield School at the end of the second part. Although Alcott's mother suggested calling the second part "Wedding Marches," Alcott chose to call it *Good Wives.* It too was quickly written, partly because she found the book less demanding now that she could fictionalize about her family, rather than trying to transform real events into satisfactory fiction. She started composing *Good Wives* on November 1, 1868, one month after the first part was published. By January, 1869, it too was published, also by Roberts Brothers of Boston.

Alcott's uniqueness.   *Little Women* was quite different from any other children's book of the time. Frank Preston Stearns notes that, with the exception of the Tom Brown books by Thomas Hughes, at that period there were no books for adolescents, especially for those between the ages of fifteen and twenty.[3] By modern standards the March girls seem to act considerably younger than that, and the story is tame compared to adolescent fiction today. But for its time the book was unique in American children's literature.

Though there were other books for younger girls and an abundance of domestic fiction by other women writers whose examples Alcott might follow, she was also careful to avoid their literary clichés. When Jo, her own counterpart in the novel, tries writing for children, Alcott comments that "much as she liked to write for children, Jo could not consent to depict all her naughty boys as being eaten by bears or tossed by mad bulls, because they did not go to a particular Sabbath school, nor all the good infants, who did go, as rewarded by every kind of bliss, from gilded gingerbread to escorts of angels, when they departed this life with psalms or sermons on their lisping tongues."[4] Like Jo, Alcott would not resort to the preachiness and heavy-handed didacticism of the stories published by the American Sunday School Union or the American Tract Society, publishers of popular religious literature for children. She even avoided the less sectarian moralizing of the "Oliver Optic" books. Though *Little Women* may seem preachy to us today, it does so only because of Alcott's intention to resolve the difficulties of moral conduct in a confusing world of peer pressure, parental guidance, and conscience. A code of right behavior is implicit here, but the author does not intrude to point a finger at the reader and preach, as other writers for children did at that time. Instead, she demonstrates to the reader what is right moral action by posing a situation with believable characters trying to puzzle out the answers for themselves.

In *Little Women* Alcott also avoids taking up the political and ethical causes that characterized some children's literature of the time. Her family was deeply involved in current political reform movements, but as much as Alcott herself supported women's suffrage, the abolition of slavery, the temperance movement, and educational reform, and various programs for social welfare, these interests appear in the book only indirectly, not as major themes. Meg makes Laurie pledge not to drink at her wedding;

Amy is removed from school because her parents do not approve of corporal punishment; Jo laments her lot as a girl and envies the freedom of boys. The Marches give generously to the immigrant Hummel family, and Meg hires the oldest Hummel daughter as a domestic servant after her marriage. But the story is not written as a fable to prove the validity of any of the Alcotts' intellectual and political ideas.

Alcott learned her lesson after the reception of her novel *Moods* (1864), a book which is full of ideas about marriage and the social consequences of divorce. After the critics' complaints, she determined that "my next book shall have no *ideas* in it, only facts, and the people shall be as ordinary as possible." While she was not impressed with the manuscript of *Little Women* when she finished it, by the time she was ready to write the second part of the novel, she commented in her diary, "Not a bit sensational, but simple and true"; "I now find my 'Marches' sober, nice people."[5] By not taking up any causes in the book, Alcott avoided the preachiness of the contemporary Sunday School type of literature. By not including her family's unusual political notions, she also insured the book's universality. The Marches are the all-American family; they do not talk about slavery, so that they would not offend readers in the North or the South. They are not the rather eccentric Alcotts of Concord, but fictionalized counterparts.

Alcott also avoids the extremes of the deathbed scenes popular in domestic fiction of the nineteenth century. The most famous of these is the death of little Eva, the seven-year-old angel of *Uncle Tom's Cabin* by Harriet Beecher Stowe (1852). Eva is much like Beth in *Little Women;* she is a household saint, the most spiritual of the characters in her fictional world, who leads Stowe's other characters on toward the life hereafter by first going herself. It takes her thirty pages to die. Here is the moment of death:

The child lay panting on her pillows, as one exhausted—the large clear eyes rolled up and fixed. And what said those eyes, that spoke so much of Heaven? Earth was past, and earthly pain; but so solemn, so mysterious, was the triumphant brightness of that face that it choked even the sobs of sorrow. They pressed around her in breathless stillness. . . .

"Oh, Eva, tell us what you see! What is it?" said her father.

A bright, a glorious smile passed over her face, and she said brokenly, "Oh! love,—joy,—peace!" gave one sigh and passed from death unto life!

Farewell, beloved child! the bright eternal doors have closed after thee; we shall see thy sweet face no more. Oh, woe for them who watched thy entrance into heaven, when they shall wake and find only the cold gray sky of daily life, and thou gone forever![6]

The scene is pathetic, bordering on the bathetic. Eva does not simply pass away, but wrenches herself from earth to heaven, leaving behind her a few choice, prophetic words. As if the scene were not overwritten by itself, Stowe liberally sprinkles the narrative with exclamation points to add even more emotion.

This example, with many others like it, stood before Alcott as she wrote about the death of her own sister Lizzie. The death scene is certainly foreshadowed; Beth is so pure that real life does not seem to be nearly good enough for her from the very beginning of the book. But in spite of Alcott's skill in creating theatrical scenes, as shown in her short stories for adults, in *Little Women* she avoids the extremes of sentimentality evident in most of the deathbed incidents in the literature of her time: "Seldom, except in books, do the dying utter memorable words, see visions, or depart with beatified countenances: and those who have sped many parting souls know that to most the end comes as naturally as sleep. As Beth had hoped, the 'tide went out easily;' and in the dark hour before the dawn, on the bosom where she had drawn her first breath, she quietly drew her last, with no farewell but one loving look, one little sigh." Alcott had set the scene with all the sentimental equipment of the sentimental deathbed: " . . . the flowers were up fair and early, and the birds came back in time to say good-by to Beth. . . ." She even makes Beth, who is eighteen years old at the time of her death, into a child again, to increase the pathos: "Beth . . . like a tired but trustful child, clung to the hands that had led her all her life . . ." (446). But rather than portray Beth as a prescient, precious little angel, full of divine sentences for all occasions, including her own death, Alcott avoids the conventions of the literature of her time. She lets Beth go without final words of farewell. It is a tribute to her restraint that she wrote about such a tearful scene without filling it with undue emotion.

Beth leaves behind her Jo, who is lonely and does not know what to do with her life after her sister's death. Again Alcott chooses an original path for Jo, one that is more realistic than the clichéd behavior of the women in other sentimental novels of the time: "Now, if she had been the heroine of a moral story-book, she ought at this period of her life to have become quite saintly, renounced the world, and gone about doing good in a mortified bonnet, with tracts in her pocket. But, you see, Jo wasn't a heroine; she was only a struggling human girl, like hundreds of others, and she just acted out her nature, being sad, cross, listless, or energetic, as the mood suggested" (463). Slowly Jo gets over her grief, not by avoiding it in a highly improbable course of action, but by grappling with it day by day, "learning to do her duty" (464). Jo may be a sentimental heroine, but she is not a stereotype; instead she is flesh and blood and must live in a real world outside the storybook lives of other heroines.

The most unconventional occurrence in the whole book is Jo's refusal to marry Laurie. After the publication of the first half of the book, when her readers wrote to ask her to tell them how the March sisters married, Alcott became indignant: "Girls write to ask me who the little women marry, as if that was the one and only aim of a woman's life. I won't marry Jo to Laurie to please any one."[7] Jo and Laurie are the two most interesting people in the novel and seem eminently suitable for each other, as romantic heroes and heroines usually are. But Alcott defies such a simple, sentimental ending. Jo's explanation to Laurie why she refuses to marry him may not convince the reader: "You and I are not suited to each other, because our quick tempers and strong wills would probably make us very miserable" (388). Thus far in the book, the two have been such close friends and interesting characters exactly because of their "quick tempers and strong wills." But Jo's more telling argument is much more convincing since Alcott herself believed it: "I don't believe I shall ever marry. I'm happy as I am, and love my liberty too well to be in any hurry to give it up for any mortal man" (389). Alcott pairs Laurie off with Amy, in a traditional ending for a romantic novel about marriage, but she seems willing to let Jo go on as an unconventional heroine, a spinster but still happy and fulfilled.

However, Alcott finally bows to the wishes of her convention-dominated readers and does marry Jo to Professor Bhaer. But a less conventional romantic interest could hardly be found. Amy comments about Professor Bhaer in the novel, "I do wish he was a little younger and a good deal richer" (484), and so do most readers. But it is not sheer obstinacy that impelled Alcott to pair off Jo with the Professor. The marriage might not be the most romantically advantageous, but it has other assets. It gives Jo the freedom to be more than just a housewife. She and the Professor found the Plumfield School, and in its educational atmosphere they maintain an intellectual quality in their relationship that is clearly lacking in the more traditional marriages of Meg and John Brooke and Amy and Laurie. While it may be argued that Alcott failed artistically because she was not able to withstand the pressure to marry Jo off and instead portray her as a happy, independent spinster, it is also true that marrying Jo to Laurie would have satisfied the readers but not the more intellectually minded Miss Alcott.

The girls themselves are also unique in the children's literature of the time, for they are not perfect, but neither are they wholly depraved. Many of the books contemporary with *Little Women* present children as being totally good or totally bad, but never in-between. The reader needs only to turn to Martha Finley Farquharson's *Elsie Dinsmore* (1868), published in the same year as *Little Women*, to see the difference. Elsie is a saint, a Christian among cannibals who constantly beset her in the most hideous and perverse ways. In contrast, the March sisters, perhaps with the exception of Beth, are quite human and faulty. In fact, it is the girls' faults and their attempts to improve upon them that keep the book going. And even at the end of the second part, the reader knows that the girls have become "Good Wives" but not perfect ones; they are certainly not candidates for canonization. They are the first "naughty" children allowed to survive and prosper in American children's literature. After them comes a long line of literary children who are accepted and loved in spite of their faults: Katy Carr in *What Katy Did* by Susan Coolidge (1872); Tom Bailey in *The Story of a Bad Boy* by Thomas Bailey Aldrich (1870); and most important, Mark Twain's *Tom Sawyer* (1876) and *Huckleberry Finn* (1884).

Along with their imperfections of behavior is their imperfection of language, about which some contemporary critics complained. Today the way the girls speak seems above reproach, with the exception of Amy's malapropisms. But at the time children in children's books spoke formally, always in complete sentences with proper subordination and parallelisms. In fact, they were capable of uttering complete paragraphs spontaneously, without hesitation or interruption. For Jo to exclaim "Christopher Columbus" was inexcusable slang, as it seems to Amy. But Alcott knew how to portray real children and so had her characters speak colloquially. She captured the real voices of children and young people in her writing, for the first time in the history of American children's literature.

The moral tone of the book is undoubtedly high, and Alcott constantly inculcates moral and religious values, although she does not press any narrow sectarian interests on her readers as many other authors of the time did. But God is definitely a character in this book. When Marmee is speaking to Jo about learning to control her temper, she explains that there is a source of help for her that is more powerful than anything that her earthly parents can give her: "My child, the troubles and temptations of your life are beginning, and may be many; but you can overcome and outlive them all if you learn to feel the strength and tenderness of your

Heavenly Father as you do that of your earthly one. The more you love and trust Him, the nearer you will feel to Him, and the less you will depend on human power and wisdom. His love and care never tire or change, can never be taken from you, but may become the source of life-long peace, happiness, and strength" (87). The emphasis here is clearly on the spiritual side of life in a rather conventional way.

But this conventionality is undercut by Alcott's insistence on cataloging the material pleasures of this world. As Jo says at the beginning of the book, "Christmas won't be Christmas without any presents" (1). This is clearly a spiritually misguided statement.[8] The girls learn their lesson when their love for Marmee appeals to their higher instincts and they decide to give her gifts instead of buying for themselves. Marmee then reinforces the lesson by asking them to give up their Christmas breakfast to the poor German immigrant family, the Hummels.

The Pilgrim's Progress.   The spirituality of the book is further underscored by Alcott's borrowings from John Bunyan's *The Pilgrim's Progress,* the allegory of the true Christian quest for heaven. Bunyan's story traces the journey of Christian from his home in the City of Destruction to the Celestial City, which represents heaven. Along the way he meets various allegorical characters, such as Faithful, Evangelist, and Worldly Wiseman, who either help or hinder him on his way. He also passes through such allegorical places as Vanity Fair and the Valley of Humiliation, where he learns about and tests his faith.

The Pilgrim's Progress was a particularly influential book in Alcott's life. Bronson Alcott read it frequently to his daughters, and his wife, like Mrs. March in *Little Women,* encouraged the girls to play the game of Pilgrim's Progress, packing them picnic lunches for the pilgrimages from the cellar to the top of the house, where their burdens would magically tumble off down the stairs. Alcott's parents encouraged in their daughters the deep soul-searching that one finds in Christian's tormented journey, and urged them to root out and confess all their sins, however trivial, and replace sinfulness with godly, submissive behavior.

Since *Little Women* is at least partially an autobiography, the reader would expect a book and a habit of mind as pervasive as these were in Alcott's own life to reveal themselves in the book. Alcott shows the dominance of *The Pilgrim's Progress* as a structure in *Little Women* in her preface, adapted from "The Author's Way of Sending Forth His Second Part of the 'Pilgrim'" to instruct "young damsels . . . to prize / The world which is to come, and so be wise." The title of the first chapter is "Playing Pilgrims." In this chapter Marmee reminds the sisters of their game of

Pilgrim's Progress when they were younger, and in the course of this conversation the reader is told that each girl has a burden or flaw which must be overcome as much as possible; they resolve from the very beginning to work to gain "the peace which is a true Celestial City" and to "see how far on" they "can get before father comes home" (11).

The stage is set, then, for the chapters where each sister faces the realistic equivalent of one of Christian's fantasy episodes on his pilgrimage. In chapter nine, "Meg Goes to Vanity Fair," Meg is swept away from the humble, modest home of her parents to the worldly Moffat mansion, which is full of temptations to immodest, vain behavior, such as flirting and wearing low-cut dresses and makeup. Chapter seven, "Amy's Valley of Humiliation," shows Amy's version of vanity when she tries to keep up with the clique at school by parceling out pickled limes to her friends and is caught, feruled, and publicly embarrassed by her teacher. Beth's journey is not a particularly difficult one. In the opening chapter her mother says that Beth hasn't got any burdens, as the other sisters do, but she objects: "Yes, I have; mine is dishes and dusters, and envying girls with nice pianos, and being afraid of people" (11). The burdens for her are so light that Beth finds "The Palace Beautiful" only next door in Mr. Laurence's house in chapter four.

But perhaps the most memorable grappling with burdens is in chapter eight, "Jo Meets Apollyon," when Amy, out of spite, burns Jo's manuscript; in reciprocation, Jo nearly shakes her to death and is tempted, although only momentarily, to let her take her chances with drowning. While all the other burdens become almost trivial under Alcott's nostalgic gaze back at a childhood in which her sisters succumbed to childish indulgences but never went far astray, Jo's burden of temper is the one that is most deeply felt in the book. Meg's vanity is understandable, especially when the relative poverty of her life is contrasted to the sparkling gaiety and excitement of Annie Moffat's life. Amy's humiliation is only over a schoolgirl mishap, and she is humorous in her overly dramatic rendition of her catastrophe, complete with malapropisms. And Beth is just too insubstantial in will or character for the reader to get very involved. But Jo, Alcott's re-creation of herself, has the real burden a real character deserves, and her wrestling with her anger is felt throughout the book.

Alcott's use of the events in *The Pilgrim's Progress* to characterize each sister's struggle reminds the reader that she sees each sister's fight as spiritually crucial. Amy, Meg, and Beth may seem to have somewhat charming struggles, but the nostalgic golden gaze is not the only one Alcott focuses on them. After all, when Christian and Faithful venture into Vanity Fair, Evangelist warns them that their lives will be in peril. And Faithful is in fact executed in a most horrific way. In the Valley of Humiliation Christian meets the monster Apollyon and does mortal combat with him—no ordinary garden variety monster of romance and fairy-tale tradition, but partaking of all the worst characteristics of fantasy monsters, simultaneously sea monster, dragon, bear, and lion. In spite of the loving glance backward to her childhood which sometimes causes Alcott to sentimentalize, the burdens and struggles that the March sisters face are difficult and crucial, since the spiritual well-being, the final disposition of each soul in the afterlife, depends on each sister's successful combat against will and desire. In her preface Alcott stated that the girls should "learn . . . to prize / The world which is to come, and so be wise."

The "Castles in the Air" chapter is central to understanding Alcott's overall design in using *The Progress*. In that chapter the sisters, joined by the ubiquitous Laurie, look back over their summer's program of self-improvement and forward to the rest of their lives. Jo says, "Wouldn't it be fun if all the castles in the air which we make could come true, and we could live in them?" (152). Each character in turn describes his dream world, what he or she wishes for in adulthood. Laurie wants to be a famous musician: "I'd like to settle in Germany, and have just as much music as I choose. I'm to be a famous musician myself, and all creation is to rush to hear me. . . ." Meg wants to be a lady of leisure: "I should like a lovely house, full of all sorts of luxurious things,—nice food, pretty clothes, handsome furniture, pleasant people, and heaps of money. I am to be mistress of it, and manage it as I like, with plenty of servants . . ." (152). Amy wants to be a famous artist: ". . . to be an artist, and go to Rome, and do fine pictures, and be the best artist in the whole world" (153). Jo wants to be a famous writer and "to do something splendid before I go into my castle—something heroic or wonderful, that won't be forgotten after I'm dead" (152). Beth doesn't want much except to remain a child in her parents' home; her wish is "to stay home safe with Father and Mother, and help take care of the family" (153). In this chapter are evident the high aspirations of all the characters but Beth, and their desires for worldly success and notoriety. Given the talent requisite to their wishes and their willingness to work hard, it seems largely within the realm of possibility that each could achieve his goal; the reader certainly wishes them on to their desired goals with his whole heart. After all, if one can succeed at spiritual combat, why not the earthly kind?

But the only sister to reach the Celestial City and get exactly what she wishes for is Beth, via the Valley of the Shadow. But then Beth wished for very little, and that is her reward in the end. The only way she can remain a child is to die, and so she does, guided by her mother and father to the heavenly gates. Meg's wish for luxury and leisure is tempered by her desire for John Brooke, and she settles into a modest, humble domestic arrangement much like her mother's. As attractive and beautiful as she is, she never gets much of a taste for the Moffats' world without being misled into paths of error, even after her marriage. Her role in the end is to be like her mother, after whom she is named.

Amy and Laurie suffer the same diminution of good fortune. Both give up their desires for fame and accomplishment; they even give up their desires for Europe. Perhaps their wishes are too exotic to be entirely palatable to Alcott. So Amy and Laurie moderate their desires until they are sufficiently humbled to accept each other. They marry, live happily ever after, and perform the roles of Lord and Lady Bountiful in the sequels. But one wonders at the end how vital a marriage is this after seeing their only offspring, another pale little Beth, barely hanging onto life in this world.

Jo's fate is the most difficult to accept. She has claimed earlier in the book that she does not want to marry, and yet she does marry a man who does not approve of her writing (at least not her gothic "potboilers" for the newspapers) and who hardly seems appropriate for her. She loses her aim to become a famous writer; she even loses Laurie. Finally she settles into the domestic pattern that Amy and Meg follow. Her end is the least satisfactory, since her struggles with temper and worldly success are the most ardently fought of all the sisters' battles and yet her reward only further diminishes her vitality and talent, rather than enhancing her as a full person. The only remnant of her spontaneity seems to be the two sons, Rob and Teddy, that she and the otherwise undistinguished Professor Bhaer produce. In spite of the fact that most readers of domestic fiction expect just such a happy ending, where love changes a woman's mind and where marriage is the Celestial City realized on earth, the reader leaves *Little Women* unsatisfied. After all, Alcott herself did not give up her writing to marry, and even when her artistic sister married, she did not give up her art.

The problem in the novel is that it was written without the second part of the book clearly in mind. Without the sequel *Good Wives*, the section of the book where Beth dies and the other three sisters marry, the book works as a unified whole. Father March comes home on Christmas Day, a year after the novel begins, and evaluates his daughters' year-long struggle to be like Christian in *The Pilgrim's Progress*. He is pleased with what he sees, for he finds Meg less vain, with hands spotted and callused by hard work. She is well prepared by her sacrifice of vanity to domestic duty to become John Brooke's wife. Jo is less boyish, more quiet and ladylike, and manages to show not a single spark of anger (or any other spontaneous emotion). Amy is less selfish and less concerned about her face in the mirror, and Beth is refined away to almost nothing by her illness. All in all, each girl has made some sacrifice of her own selfish will, and each shows a deeper concern for the family than for her own feelings. The pilgrimage has thus far been a success. The reader feels that some rough edges need to be worn away on each girl in the interest of self-improvement, but that the sisters are all still on their way to success in life and the Celestial City in afterlife. *The Pilgrim's Progress* motif is successfully rounded out.

But by the end of the sequel Alcott has extended the original structure of the book to include the sisters' marriages, according to her young readers' demands. This extension goes beyond autobiography, for neither she nor her artist sister had married, although the real John Brooke had already married the real Meg, and the real Beth had died. It is the fate of Amy and Jo that dissatisfies the reader, since each of them sacrifices so much of herself to return to the family nest and continue its heritage of domestic tranquillity. Jo gives up New York, money, and the chance to become a legitimate author; Amy gives up Europe and her artistic endeavors. For each, the justification for the sacrifice is the sublimation of will and desire, in good Bunyanesque and Victorian fashion, to the importance of the tranquil life and the more tangible rewards of children and kitchen. This is the same sacrifice that Christian and Christiana make when they decide to leave the City of Destruction.

But *Little Women* is realistic fiction and *The Pilgrim's Progress* a fantasy and an allegory. In getting the reader involved in the real world of the March sisters, Alcott makes the reader wish even more fervently for their success in the real world, whether in Europe, New York, or Concord; and because questions of the afterlife are not central to the story, the reader is not satisfied with the delayed religious gratification, however glorious, arranged for Christian in *The Pilgrim's Progress*. Amy and Jo must give up too much for the domestic happiness that pales beside the more substantial rewards available to them in their world. It is only by accepting the premise that happy marriage ever after is the realistic equivalent of the Celestial City in domestic fiction and by reading *Little Men* to find out about Jo's happy life that the reader finds solace at the end of *Little Women*.

All this self-sacrifice and conventionality is undercut, however, by Alcott's rewards for the girls. Though they give up their own pleasures in order to give Marmee gifts, those small offerings are reveled in, fussed over, and thoroughly enjoyed for their sensual values. Amy's rose and cologne are smelled by everyone, Beth's handkerchiefs are minutely inspected, Meg's gloves detailed carefully for their elegance, and Jo's slippers widely praised for their comfort. The girls are rewarded by a full account of the sensual pleasures that Marmee will derive from the gifts. The sacrifice of the breakfast is rewarded by an elegant supper sent in by old Mr. Laurence, replete with "ice cream,—actually two dishes of it, pink and white,— and cake and fruit and distracting French bonbons, and, in the middle of the table, four great bouquets of hothouse flowers!" (22–23). As delicious as the breakfast was, the elegance of the supper more than compensates for it.

Alcott maintains this focus on the material goods of this world throughout the novel. In spite of the Marches' genteel poverty and the girls' resolutions not to envy what they can't have and to be contented with what they do have, there are extensive, seductive passages describing items of female dress and elegancies of hospitality and fine living. The reader feels that Meg is not so very naughty when she dresses up at the Moffats in a blue silk gown with earrings and a distracting pair of French boots which even Laurie approves of, while reproaching her for being otherwise faddishly dressed. Amy's mortification at having to wear hand-me-downs is also perfectly understandable and sympathetic and inspires reader sympathy for her. The whole family enjoys the fine decorative touches on Beth's piano. For all the avid interest in the lofty, more spiritual aspects of life, *Little Women* is a very temporal, materialistic book.[9]

Wedding Marches.   The greatest upset of the traditional girls' novel is the promise Marmee holds out to her girls that they need never grow up, never leave her and this rich, satisfying world, remaining always the beloved and protected little women. The feminist critic Nina Auerbach points out that the book is not really about growing up and becoming a wife and mother. The coziness of home and Marmee's gentle spirit are so attractive that every time one of the sisters leaves the family circle, either by marriage or by death, the departure is seen as a wrenching away and a disruption of the family, rather than as a celebration of the normal processes of maturing.[10] When Marmee hears about Meg's involvement with John Brooke, she says, "It is natural and right that you should all go to homes of your own in time, but I do want to keep my girls as long as I can; and I am sorry that this happened so soon." Eventually Meg does marry, but Jo predicts that "Brooke will . . . carry her off, and make a hole in the family; and I shall break my heart, and everything will be abominably uncomfortable" (216). As pretty as the wedding is, the March family is unhappy; "in spite of the smiles on the motherly face, there was a secret sorrow hid in the motherly heart at the flight of the first bird from the nest" (264). And at the ceremony itself, "Mother and sisters gathered close, as if loath to give Meg up" (266). But Meg makes clear where her allegiance is even though she is married, for "the minute she was fairly married, Meg cried, 'The first kiss for Marmee!'" (267), and promises before she leaves for her new home with John that "I shall come [home to Marmee] every day . . . and expect to keep my old place in all your hearts, though I *am* married" (270). Meg is not really growing up; she's just moving next door.

Beth's death is a similar experience, in that it too is seen as a break in the family circle, no matter how much the family members try to keep her with them in their memories. Certainly this is a much more appropriate occasion for mourning, as any death is, but it follows a pattern of mourning any departure from the family, no matter how joyous the occasion.

Jo's and Amy's marriages are not as devastating as Meg's or as Beth's death; Amy's union with Laurie is really like marrying a brother already in the family. Moving in next door, Amy and Laurie also restore Beth to the family circle by naming their only child, a frail, blue-eyed blonde princess, after the departed sister. Jo marries Professor Bhaer who is in no way a match for Laurie's attractions of character, physique, or fortune. But in many ways Jo is simply marrying a father figure who will guide her as her parents have. When Bhaer woos her, he is "giving the daughter lessons in love" (498). And when they are married and happily established at Plumfield, "Jo made queer mistakes; but the wise Professor steered her safely into calmer waters" (517). The marriage is not at all a traditional one, for Jo does not turn her energies into becoming the perfect housekeeper and mother like Meg. Nor does her path become easy, as does Amy's with the benefit of Laurie's money. Jo still continues her writing, as will be seen in *Little Men* and *Jo's Boys,* the sequels to *Little Women* and *Good Wives.* And she becomes the headmistress of a school, doing much good for the children who come under her care. Plumfield becomes the site of many family reunions, as in the last scene of the book. But again the focus is on Marmee as the center of the circle, and her daughters return to her, albeit with husbands and grandchildren in tow, as the little women they will always, in essence, remain. Readers have complained bitterly since the book's publication that Jo should have married Laurie; critics have complained that Alcott's artistic vision fails because Jo marries, and rather prosaically at that, when Alcott herself remained single. She is certainly giving in to her readers' demands that the sisters marry, but in their hearts they are still Marmee's little women, returning always to her for advice and consolation.

Critical Reputation and Reevaluation.   Critically, the book has suffered much since its publication. Young readers have kept it alive, but older ones have not found the sentimentality, optimism, and simplicity of the story satisfying. Martha Saxton in Alcott's most recent biography compares *Little Women* and Alcott's first novel, *Moods,* and concludes that *Moods* is the more mature novel and that *Little Women* shows little artistry and is an artistic regression for Alcott. The characters and the situations are simplified to the point where the characters are not humanized.[11] Brigid Brophy entitles her article on *Little Women* "A Masterpiece and Dreadful" because she finds that "Alcott's characters are not challenged by the situations she devises for them, and that they do not develop, but remain statically good."[12] Readers have lost much of their taste for the sentimental novel, and rather than understanding the conventions of the juvenile domestic fiction genre in which Alcott was writing, critics have judged the novel by modern criteria, especially when comparing it to her adult novels.

But there is more to *Little Women* than is perceived by the reader who sees only the sunny, simplistic patina. Marmee may *seem* all goodness and light, but she admits to having a temper which even in her adulthood she can only control and not conquer. On occasion this temper rises to the surface. For instance, in the chapter "Experiments," the March sisters decide that for their summer vacation they will not work at their housekeeping chores, but will while away the time as they please. The girls find the first few days boring and even irritating, but Marmee goes along with their plan, doing their chores for them. At the end of the first week, however, Mrs. March decides to back out of the arrangement and leave the girls to their own devices; as Meg reports, "Mother isn't sick, only very tired, and she says she is going to stay quietly in her room all day, and let us do the best we can. It's a very queer thing for her to do, she does n't act a bit like herself; but she says it had been a hard week for her, so we must n't grumble, but take care of ourselves" (118). In the afternoon Mrs. March goes out visiting, again leaving the girls. If she had wanted to teach them a lesson about industry, she might just as well have let their chores go undone at the beginning of the week rather than at the end, when they have learned that Marmee will do them for them. Her willingness to desert the girls in this manner does not sound like the loving, forgiving, even-tempered Marmee, and she even manages a kind of "I told you so" after the experiment is over: "Are you satisfied with your experiment, girls, or do you want another week of it?" (124).

Alcott's manner of dealing with her father in the novel also raises some problems. Neither Louisa nor Bronson Alcott understood the other very well, for they were total opposites in personality, as can be gathered from their respective writings. Bronson was a philosopher and tran-scendentalist, Louisa a writer of realistic and domestic fiction. While Bronson's books meditated on large, abstract topics, Louisa wrote about practical, down-to-earth concerns. Though they undoubtedly admired and loved each other, there was a certain distance in their relationship, fostered by their great differences in personality.

In *Little Women* Louisa gives the Marches' father (Bronson) an admirable vocation as a clergyman, and sends him off to the Civil War, a journey which she herself made in reality as a nurse. Thus he is kept offstage until the very end of the first half of the novel. He reappears on Christmas Day, one year after the novel's opening, to hand out praise for the girls' domestic accomplishments in their struggles with their burdens. He of course finds them much improved and congratulates them all. But much as Mr. March has been an important force in the novel, inspiring the girls to continue their struggles in his absence, he is a real presence in none of the March family sagas. The reader never sees him acting out his role as a clergyman. Nor does he give much advice to the daughters, since they turn to Marmee rather than Father when troubled. His shadowy presence indicates simul-taneously the great admiration Louisa had for her father and the strained tenor of their relationship which made sending him off to the Civil War the only way that she could deal (or not deal) with him.

Jo's relationship with Amy is also a difficult one. Alcott's sister May was the youngest in the family, so young that she did not understand the turmoil of Alcott's early years as a struggling author and teacher, or the near-catastrophe of the Fruitlands experiment. May was the talented, amiable baby of the family who always seemed to get what she wanted. The tension in their relationship is evident in the chapter "Jo Meets Apollyon," where Amy spites Jo by burning her manuscript, and Jo retaliates by nearly letting Amy drown. Sibling rivalry is a problem for nearly every set of sisters, but the rivalry here has reached unusually violent proportions, to the point where Amy nearly dies. In spite of the fact that Jo loves her sister, the tempers here which were present in real life are nearly out of control, in spite of Alcott's efforts elsewhere to present a happy, helpful, loving family portrait.

Perhaps Alcott is not as simplistic as she might otherwise seem. Her family life had been difficult. Although she was writing from an autiobiographical inspiration, she was, after all, writing fiction. Life is never as simple as it is in the sentimental novel, and in spite of her willingness to comply with the requirements of the genre, Alcott does not so alter her family that the difficulties do not come through. She could transmogrify her father into an honorable and wise clergyman. She could change her sisters' ages so that they would be adolescents and not the young women that they were when many of the events took place. She could even fantasize marriages that had not happened and children who would never be born. But she remained true to life in showing not only the profound love that she had for her family, but also the more unpleasant sides of their characters.

Little Men

Little Men (1871) followed *Little Women* by two years. In it Alcott continues the March family saga, focusing on the Plumfield school that Jo and Professor Bhaer had founded at the end of *Little Women* five years earlier. The same characters are clustered around the fringes of Plumfield—the Laurences, the Brookes, and Marmee and Father. The grandchildren, Daisy and Demi, Rob and Teddy, and Little Beth, in attendance at the harvest celebration at the end of *Little Women,* are also present, although they are now old enough to go to the Bhaers' school. There are also some additions, namely, the other student boarders, to round out the story. Again Alcott employs an episodic technique, a chapter devoted almost exclusively to one pupil at a time, to trace the growth of these students from the planting of the seeds of virtue in each in the spring, to the harvesting of the fruits at the Thanksgiving festival at the book's close.

Daisy is the same domestic angel she was in *Little Women,* absolutely devoted to her twin brother Demi, who has turned out to be a bookish young lad, still interested in knowing how things work. Teddy is Mrs. Jo's loving baby who lets everyone love and kiss him, even though that loving gets him into trouble at times. Rob, his older brother, is "an energetic morsel of a boy, who seemed to have discovered the secret of perpetual motion,"[13] sometimes leading him to act before he thinks. And little Bess, Laurie's and Amy's only daughter, is the little blonde princess of the story who is worshiped by all the boys of the school and whose adoration inspires them to greater exhibitions of cleanliness and good manners. Emil and Franz are Mr. Bhaer's nephews, the senior scholars at the school. Meg, John, Laurie, May, Mr. and Mrs. March, and Mr. Laurence show up in the narrative as well, but the story focuses mainly on the young people who attend Plumfield.

The non-family members at Plumfield include Stuffy Cole, who is overweight; Dolly Pettingill, who is rather undistinguished in any way; Jack Ford, a cheat; Ned Barker, who is clumsy; Billy Ward, a retarded boy; and Dick Brown, a hunchback; as a group these are stock characters and therefore remain undeveloped in the course of the novel. But four other boys receive sharper focus—Tommy Bangs, the happy prankster and arsonist; Nat Blake, the poor street musician who loves his music but sometimes tells lies; Naughty Nan, the girl who wants to be a boy but decides to learn doctoring instead; and Dan Kean, the bad boy who nearly ruins the Bhaers' successful score in reforming boys. These four, along with Daisy and Demi, and sometimes Rob and Teddy, form the nucleus of Plumfield School and have most of the adventures.

Gravestones.   Alcott returned to the March family when she heard while in Italy that John Pratt, husband of her sister Anna and father of her two nephews, had died. She claimed to write so that the children's futures would be made secure and comfortable by the profits from the book's sale. In reality, John Pratt had already provided for his family; Louisa was simply helping her family along out of habit. But in the book she does memorialize John Pratt in John Brooke in a way that no one else did. Without *Little Men,* his name would not be known today.

She describes her brother-in-law in her eulogistic report of Mr. Brooke's funeral, one of the central episodes in this book:

One would have said that modest John Brooke, in his busy, quiet, humble life, had had little time to make friends, but now they seemed to start up everywhere—old and young, rich and poor, high and low, for all unconsciously his influence had made itself widely felt, his virtues were remembered, and his hidden charities rose up to bless him. The group about his coffin was a far more eloquent eulogy than any Mr. March could utter. There were the rich men whom he had served faithfully for years, the poor old women whom he cherished with his little store, in memory of his mother, the wife to whom he had given such happiness that death could not mar it utterly, the brothers and sisters in whose hearts he had made a place forever, the little son and daughter, who already felt the loss of his strong arm and tender voice, the young children, sobbing for their kindest playmate, and the tall lads, watching with softened faces a scene which they never could forget. (304–5)

As much as Alcott had disapproved of Anna's marriage to John Pratt, she sincerely mourned his passing. If she did not need to provide her family with financial security through writing the book, she did need to write in order to express her grief.

The Educational Novel and Bronson Alcott.   *Little Men* is an educational novel in the tradition of the boys' school story established by Thomas Hughes's *Tom Brown at Rugby* (1857) and *Tom Brown at Oxford* (1861). But *Little Men* does not imitate Hughes's pedagogy, for this is the story of Bronson Alcott's educational ideas worked out in a realistic setting. There are some clear parallels between Plumfield School and Bronson's Temple School (1834–40). For example, at the end of *Little Women* Plumfield is said to have had as a pupil "a merry little quadroon, who could not be taken in elsewhere, but who was welcome to the 'Bhaer-garten,' though some people predicted that his admission would ruin the school" (518). Though Bronson Alcott's advanced educational ideas led many parents to withdraw their children from the Temple School, it was his admission of a black girl that finally led to its closing.

Bronson also believed in the education of the body, as well as of the mind and spirit. The Bhaers follow Bronson's pattern by encouraging the boys to play cricket and to work in their gardens. Although this is the story of a school, the reader seldom sees the children in the classroom, nor does he see the Professor conducting a class on the more conventional subjects one would expect in a school, though the reader is assured that the pupils do study reading, writing, arithmetic, history, and natural sciences. But as Alcott says, "The lessons were short, and there were many holidays, for the Bhaers believed in cultivating healthy bodies by much exercise" (145).

Billy Ward is the object lesson against pushing children too fast intellectually. Although he is thirteen years old with the understanding of a six-year-old, he had formerly been quite precocious. But "his father had hurried him on too fast, giving him all sorts of hard lessons, keeping him at his books six hours a day, and expecting him to absorb knowledge as a Strasburg goose does the food crammed down its throat." Billy contracts a fever, and when he recovers, his "mind was like a slate over which a sponge has passed, leaving it blank" (23). The Bhaers are careful to balance their curriculum, cultivating both body and mind. They don't wish Demi to spend all his time in books, nor will they let Dan roam in the field and avoid his lessons; happily Demi and Dan pair off, each benefiting the other by sharing the knowledge gained in books and in nature.

The Bhaers, like Bronson Alcott, also believe in cultivating the spirit as well as the intellect. Mr. Bhaer in good transcendentalist fashion takes his pupils on Sunday afternoon walks in the fields and meadows, where they find "sermons in stones, books in the running brooks, and good in every thing" (32). The higher faculties are also cultivated by Mrs. Jo's "conscience book," where she records the actions of her pupils for the week and discusses her report with each of them on Sunday night. Bronson took his daughters for walks; he also kept extensive notes on their progress, both educational and moral, especially on his elder daughters, Anna and Louisa. And both he and his wife read the girls' diaries and commented on what they found in them, either praising and encouraging them, or admonishing them to do better. For everyday discipline the Alcotts also resorted to writing, as Mrs. Jo does. The Alcotts reprimanded their daughters, but they never did so in public; rather they recalled the faults to the girls later, usually in writing. Since Alcott considered that she and her sisters had turned out quite well, she incorporated Bronson's method of discipline into her novel; all the pupils there likewise turn out well.

Bronson Alcott resorted to this rather indirect approach to discipline because he, like almost no one else at his time, did not believe in corporal punishment. This idea too is worked out in the novel. Nat Blake gives in to his besetting sin and tells a lie; the first time Professor Bhaer lets him off with a warning; the next time, however, the Professor resorts to punishing Nat by having him thrash the Professor. The Professor reports that his grandmother punished his own lying by cutting off the tip of his tongue with scissors, a not unusual punishment in nineteenth-century America. He says approvingly, "that was terrible, you may believe, but it did me much good" (56). The reader is relieved that Nat will not have to undergo the same punishment, but for Nat and the other boys the idea of striking the kind and good Professor is equally horrifying. Emil, the Professor's nephew, reports that when the Professor used the same punishment on him, "I was hopping mad at the time and thought I shouldn't mind a bit, rather like it perhaps. But when I'd hit Uncle one good crack, everything he had ever done for me came into my head all at once, somehow, and I couldn't go on! No sir! if he'd laid me down and walked on me, I wouldn't have minded, I felt so mean. . ." (59–60).

Though this sort of punishment is quite effective in stopping undesirable behavior, neither Bronson, Louisa, nor the Professor seemed to realize that it also imposes a terrible burden of guilt on the child who has to strike his parent or parent-surrogate. Knowing that he faces this kind of punishment, the child also loses his option to be angry, either at his parent or at the circumstances which brought him to do the naughty deed. It also means that the parent cannot be angry, but must submit to the punishment without showing any emotion but disappointment toward the disobedient child. All in all, Bronson's ideas about discipline did not lead to an understanding, healthy and free of tension, between parent and child about what behavior was expected and what forbidden; his methods could only have brought about an anxiety and an unresolvable tension in a family so regulated.

Finally, both Bronson and Louisa, as shown in *Little Men,* believed in coeducation, although Bronson was not as ardent a supporter of equal education opportunities as was his daughter. The coeducation begins in a small way because Daisy is the only girl at the school, there primarily because she and Demi will not allow themselves to be separated. But Daisy "is getting prim and Bettyish and needs stirring up a bit" (107), as her Aunt Jo says, lest she become entirely too complacent and passive in her housewifely ways. So the Bhaers invite the neighborhood tomboy, naughty Nan Harding, to live at the school. Nan is a girl much like Louisa Alcott was. As Mrs. Jo says, "I feel a great sympathy for Nan, because I was such a naughty child myself that I know all about it" (107). Like Alcott, Nan can run faster than any of the boys and is eager to show them that she can do almost anything they can. When Professor and Mrs. Bhaer turn Nan's attention to her studies, "the lads had to do their best to keep their places, for Nan showed them that girls could do most things as well as boys, and some things better" (116–17). Alcott is even more sympathetic to Nan than she was to her own character Jo in *Little Women,* for she gives Nan the guidance she needs to take up a likely profession, medicine. Jo may have determined not to marry but to do "something splendid," most likely as an author; but her marriage to the Professor diverts her attention from her career. Nan, like Jo, vows not to be tied down: "I don't want any house to fuss over. I shall have an office, with lots of bottles and drawers and pestle things in it, and I shall drive round in a horse and chaise and cure sick people. That will be such fun" (242–43). In *Jo's Boys,* sequel to *Little Men,* the reader finds that Alcott has not tampered with Nan's destiny as a happy spinster-doctor, but rather has let her fulfill her desires in a way that was not permitted to Jo March or Jo March Bhaer.

Alcott's feminist leanings here do not mean that Nan and Daisy can ignore housewifely accomplishments, however. Mrs. Jo buys a toy cookstove and gives both Nan and Daisy cooking lessons. Both girls help in the kitchen preparing the great Thanksgiving feast that closes the book. They both can sew, and Nan's skill as a healer, using the herbs in her garden and her native skill, makes her a particularly desirable companion to the boys. Alcott also saw that coeducation not only benefited the girls, but the boys as well. Her original argument for bringing Nan to the school was that it would be good since the boys "must learn gentle ways and improve their manners, and having girls about will do it better than any thing else" (106). Nan, too, must learn these gentle ways, and does, following the examples of Mrs. Jo and Daisy.

Little Men stands as a monument to Bronson Alcott's educational theories and methods. Louisa praises Bronson by praising his successful pupils. Mr. March, Bronson's surrogate in the novel, seldom appears although Demi quotes him frequently. Indeed, Demi is his grandfather's greatest success story:

Demi was one of the children who show plainly the effect of intelligent love and care, for soul and body worked harmoniously together. . . . Grandfather March cultivated the little mind with the tender wisdom of a modern Pythagoras—not tasking it with long, hard lessons, parrot-learned, but helping it to unfold as naturally and beautifully as sun and dew help roses bloom. He was not a perfect child, by any means, but his faults were of the better sort, and being early taught the secret of self-control, he was not left at the mercy of appetites and passions, as some poor little mortals are, and then punished for yielding to the temptations against which they have no armor. (19)

Demi benefits, as do all the pupils of Plumfield, from Bronson Alcott's seemingly simple educational dictum that the teachers' "rules were few and sensible, and the boys, knowing that they tried to make things easy and happy, did their best to obey" (18).

In fact, all the students improve dramatically over the course of the summer, and Mrs. Jo is satisfied with her harvest as she looks about her on Thanksgiving Day. All the children help in one way or another to supply the meal; they then put on a grand show for the invited guests and finally have an old-fashioned dance. The Thanksgiving at the end of the book celebrates not only the improvements in the individual boys and girls, but also the cohesiveness of Plumfield and its family. Mrs. Jo remarks, "if men and women would only trust, understand, and help one another as my children do, what a capital place the world would be!" (352). Plumfield stands not only as a successful educational experiment, but also as a utopian social experiment.

Critical Reputation.   The book is charming. Like Marmee's home in *Little Women*, Plumfield lures all its residents back to it, one way or another, and keeps them there under the guidance of the Bhaers. But, like *Little Women*, the placid surface of *Little Men* is disturbed by some darker rumblings of human emotion than might at first be evident.[14] The reader might expect to find in a school story much cavorting and high-spirited prankstering, and so he does in *Little Men*. But some of what goes on cannot be explained away by labeling the events as the result of youthful high-spiritedness.

The darkest example of the other side of Plumfield is Dan Kean, a street orphan, deserted by his mother and abused by his father, and obliged to make his way on the streets by himself. He is described when he first appears as "a most unprepossessing boy, who slouched in and stood looking about him, with a half bold, half sullen look." What is so disturbing about Dan is not so much that he borders on the incorrigible, for the Bhaers are elsewhere so optimistic and so successful with their other pupils that the reader expects that they will not fail here either; it is Mrs. Jo's attitude toward the boy, making up her mind "after one glance: 'A bad specimen, I am afraid.'" Perhaps the reader thinks that the Bhaers would take any needy boys into their school, but Mrs. Jo explains to Nat that Dan cannot simply expect to be admitted to the school because he thinks he might like to stay: "I have to choose them, because there are so many." She gives the excuse that "I have not room for them all. I wish I had" (85). Mrs. Jo is something of an elitist and may not be as sympathetic to poor boys in general as she claims to be.

She decides to take Dan on trial. She and the Professor find him pugilistic and generally a bad influence on the other boys. He starts a fist fight with Emil and scares the pet cow around the countryside by playing bull-fight with her. The Bhaers overlook his misbehavior this time, and he stays on at the school. But then Dan hosts a forbidden midnight party, complete with card games, cigars, and beer. Mrs. Jo and the Professor are horrified: "Now, of all things, Mr. Bhaer hated drinking, gambling, and swearing" (103), and they feel forced to send him away from Plumfield.

But Dan comes back, as all good children do in the March family books, seduced by the Bhaers' past kindnesses to him. But there may be more than simple kindness and affection between Mrs. Jo and Dan. Dan's description sounds much like Alcott's description of the love interests in her adult works: ". . . how tall and strong he had grown, how full of energy his face was, with its eager eyes and resolute mouth" (260). Here are the romantic interests of Alcott's adult works, Adam Warwick of *Moods,* David Sterling of *Work,* and John the blacksmith of *Hospital Sketches,* only in this case the hero is only a boy. Dan also sounds suspiciously like Henry David Thoreau in his talents as a naturalist; when he returns from his wanderings, he brings "his old straw hat stuck full of butterflies and beetles, picked up on his way; birds' eggs, carefully done up in moss, curious shells and stones, bits of fungus, and several little crabs . . ." (154–55). Thoreau was one of Louisa's lifelong though impossible passions. Once more she creates the tantalizing but unrealizable love interest.

There is a peculiar energy in the fictional relationship that cannot be explained away by an author's interest in a sympathetic character. When Dan returns, ill and hungry, Mrs. Jo comforts him in the night: "Mrs. Jo stooped to turn the pillow and smooth the bedclothes, when, to her great surprise, Dan put his arm around her neck, drew her face down to his, and kissed her, with a broken 'Thank you, ma'am . . .'" (153). Jo assumes the same comforting posture that Alcott's fictional heroines maintain over the deathbeds of their men. Jo welcomes Dan into the family again by promising him, "'You shall be my oldest son,' and she sealed her promise with a kiss that made Dan hers entirely" (198). When Dans finds in himself the need to run away from home which he can only control by running around Plumfield in circles to expend the energy, Mrs. Jo says, "don't run far, and come back to me soon, for I want you very much" (261). It is no wonder that the Professor calls Dan a "Berserker" (264), since all the romantic attention Dan gets stimulates him but gives him no outlet. The emotions portrayed in *Little Men* appear to be simple and easily resolved, but at second glance they are not always so quickly disposed of.

These perverse and twisted feelings show up in other places too. In spite of the happy home atmosphere, the younger children have some peculiar fantasies. Rob tells this story when the pupils are gathered around the fire for storytelling: "Once a lady had a million children, and one nice little boy. She went upstairs and said, 'you mustn't go in the yard.' But he wented and fell into the pump and was drowned dead. . . . She pumped him up, and wrapped him in a newspaper and put him on a shelf to dry for seed" (327–28). For a boy with a mother as perfect as Mrs. Jo, Rob has particularly violent feelings for her in his fantasies. In spite of their love for him, Nan and Daisy nearly kill baby Teddy: "Once he was shut into a closet for a dungeon and forgotten by the girls, who ran off to some out-of-door game. Another time he was half drowned in the bathtub, playing be a 'cunning little whale.' And, worst of all, he was cut down just in time after being hung up for a robber" (129).

Nan is an abundant source of unmotherly feeling, for she dresses one of her dolls as an Indian who "tomahawked all the other dolls and caused the nursery to run red with imaginary gore" (116). While Daisy is busy mothering her children, Alcott, through an aside on Nan's behavior, indicates that affection is not always what mothers feel for their children; for when Nan abandons her dolls, she is "unconsciously expressing the desire of many older ladies who cannot dispose of their families so easily, however" (24). And the Kitty-Mouse, a demon invented by Demi, demands that he, Daisy, and Teddy, "must all bring the things that we like best and burn them," including Daisy's favorite doll who "squirms" most grotesquely, and Teddy's toy village, including its "family mansion" and "one wretched little churn-shaped lady" (121–22). Again there is this perverse nature in the children that makes them act out what is otherwise unarticulated in the novel, the darker and more difficult side of human emotion and family life, the feelings that destroy rather than maintain all that is good in this fictional world.

Jo's Boys

Louisa Alcott returned to the March family a last time in *Jo's Boys* (1886). The novel was composed at widely spaced intervals because of her increasingly poor health. It was publicized fifteen years after *Little Men;* in the interval Alcott had written several other juvenile novels, had published her adult novel *Work* (1873), and had rewritten *Moods* and had it reissued (1881). She had written many short stories and collected several volumes of them from magazines such as *St. Nicholas* and *The Youth's Companion.*

It was evidently quite painful for her to return to the Marches after such a long time; the fact that she could write short stories but could not manage to face the manuscript for *Jo's Boys* attests to her difficulties. Several of those who had posed as models for the Marches were now dead; the originals for Marmee, Amy, and Mr. Laurence were gone, so that writing about them simply renewed Alcott's mourning for her mother, her sister, and Emerson. John Brooke had already been laid to rest in the pages of *Little Men,* but his absence in the Alcott family continued to be felt even fifteen years later.

The valetudinarianism of *Jo's Boys* is evident from the first page. Mrs. Jo is jubilant over the "wonderful changes" that have taken place over the past ten years, between the end of *Little Men* and the beginning of *Jo's Boys.* Mr. Laurence at his death endowed a college that stands next to Plumfield. Mrs. Jo indirectly recalls the "castles in the air" scene in *Little Women* by remembering when as children the girls used to believe in fairies and each would make three wishes. Though it does not seem that her original dream to do something "wonderful and splendid" has been accomplished, she does feel as if the fairies have granted her wishes: "Money, fame, and plenty of work I love." But Mrs. Meg remembers that the family circle, so warmly portrayed in *Little Women,* is not complete: "If dear Marmee, John, and Beth were here, it would be quite perfect." The two sisters look out, "surveying the pleasant scene before them with mingled sad and happy thoughts."[15] There is a pervasive sense of finality in this book. It is Alcott's farewell novel to her juvenile audience, and the summing up leaves the reader with mixed emotions.

   Reprise: The Educational Novel and Bronson Alcott.   The book shows the successes of Bronson Alcott's educational regime as it was established in *Little Men.* Because the earlier book showed the children for such a short time, from one spring until the following fall, it is difficult to know whether the goal of making the pupils into good men and women has been realized, whether the seeds sown will take root as perennials and not just die after a single season. Though the book concludes with many successful careers and marriages for the pupils, it is not always clear that the students have become successful adults solely because of their education.

   Certainly this is the case for Demi, Daisy, and Nan, whose stories take up the first third of the book. Demi was always Grandfather March's star pupil; he decides to apprentice himself to a publisher, Mr. Tiber, modeled after Alcott's own editor, Thomas Niles. Though book learning was never the foremost objective in Bronson Alcott's educational scheme, it was still an important one, and Demi's willingness to devote his life to books indicates that his early lessons have taken root. Daisy has always been a "little woman"; she waits around for her beloved Nat Blake to return, improved and worthy of her love. She was always a well-behaved child, never presenting any serious challenge to Bronson's theories. Nan's success as a doctor is a direct result of her education. Under Mrs. Jo's tutelage she has chosen a route unlike any other girl in the story—to be a spinster and a doctor. Although other girls in Alcott's stories have remained single at the end of their respective novels—Maud Shaw in *An Old-Fashioned Girl* and Molly Bemis in *Jack and Jill*—they remain so not to pursue careers but to take care of their aging fathers. And their happy spinsterhoods are only reported, not demonstrated in the book. Nan's career is actively under way long before the book ends. She is the only real career woman that Alcott shows in her novels, and she is a product of the educational system in *Little Women.*

   The second third of the novel is devoted to Nat, Emil, and Dan, each of whom leaves Plumfield School and takes his chances with the world far removed from Plumfield. Nat goes to Germany to finish off his musical education and to see if he has the talent to make his living and a reputation as a violinist. Unfortunately, he runs into some fashionable company and finds himself sadly in debt. Emil sails away as an officer aboard a ship that founders in mid-ocean; the captain's illness leaves him in charge of his lifeboat, containing not only the captain and his wife and daughter, but also a number of unruly tars. Dan goes west to seek his fortune, but gets caught in a crooked card game and kills a man in self-defense. In each case, the young man in question is sustained not by the educational principles of "self-knowledge, self-help, and self-control" (*Little Men,* 33), but by an alumnus's sentimental memory of the honor of his *alma mater.*

Each is reminded of the honor of the school by Mrs. Jo; each seeks to make her proud of him, and so suffers in his misfortune. All three of the boys find themselves in stock situations from sentimental novels; Nat is the young man in debt, Dan the young man unfairly jailed, Emil the young shipwreck. It would seem that Alcott lost interest in their situations, and rather than creating scenes for them that would really have challenged their moral fibre and their education, she dismisses them by playing out their fates in melodrama, having them work hard and bravely, earning their rewards, and returning to Plumfield.

In *Jo's Boys* Alcott relives her own childhood in two characters, Meg's daughter Josie, named after Jo March Bhaer, and Mrs. Jo's son Ted. Josie is an outspoken feminist. In one of the early scenes in the book she is shown in verbal combat with Ted about the talents of women. She appeals to her Grandfather March for support: "Grandpa, must women always obey men and say they are the wisest, just because they are the strongest?" Her grandfather takes her side: "Well, my dear, that is the old-fashioned belief, and it will take some time to change it. But I think the woman's hour has struck, and it looks to me as if the boys must do their best, for the girls are abreast now, and may reach the goal first. . . ."

Josie retorts to Ted: "Whole barrels of apples won't stop me when *I* start, and a dozen Teds won't trip me up, though they may try. I'll show him that a woman can act as well, if not better, than a man. It *has* been done, and will be again, and I'll never own that *my* brain isn't as good as his, though it may be smaller . . ." (33–34). Josie longs to be an actress, as Alcott herself once aspired to be, and thrills her audiences by spontaneously acting out Juliet's death scene, as Jo herself took on the more thrilling, gory parts in the plays she and her sisters produced in *Little Women.* Like Alcott herself, Josie's talents lie in character parts, as she shows in the plays at Plumfield. She takes the advice of a famous actress whom she meets and finishes her education first. At the end of the book Alcott reports that Josie is a success on the stage, although she is not permitted the luxury of Nan's spinsterhood to pursue her career, for she does marry.

Teddy is like Alcott in that he is the repository of "all the faults, whims, aspirations, and fun" (4) of Mrs. Jo's own childhood. He also has uncontrollable fits of temper, as Jo did when she faced her Apollyon in *Little Women*. The results are similar, for as Jo's anger endangered Amy's life, so Ted's endangers his brother Rob. Ted teases a dog to the point where the dog, in desperation, bites Rob as the nearest available object. It is not clear whether the dog is rabid, so Rob's wounds must be cauterized, a procedure which is so unpleasant that it causes Ted to faint while looking on. The same kind of violence erupts among the children here as it did among the earlier generation of *Little Women*. Oddly enough, Ted becomes in adulthood "an eloquent and famous clergyman, to the great delight of his astonished mother" (357–58). Ted's career is an odd one, though honorable; it seems like an afterthought on Alcott's part, for Ted has shown no particular predilection for the religious life. Perhaps Alcott had filled all the possible choices of life with her other boys; clergyman was left over, so she gave it to Ted.

Reprise: Dan Kean.   The character of Dan remains the most difficult and yet the most interesting in the novel. His seductive sexuality is even more apparent than in *Little Men;* the servant girl finds Dan "big and black, and cool as cucumbers" (58). He cuts a most romantic figure at the school dance in a Mexican costume, in contrast to all the sedately dressed young men in ties and tails. Mrs. Jo recognizes that Dan's presence has excited the interest of many of the young female collegians at Laurence College and says that she is glad "he's going away. He's too picturesque to have here among so many romantic girls. Afraid his 'grand, gloomy, and peculiar' style will be too much for our simple maids" (93). He goes west to seek his fortune, with the rather vague idea of founding Dansville, a utopian community where "there won't be much sickness . . . everyone will lead such active, wholesome lives, and only energetic young people will go there." But in spite of all this healthiness, Dansville is full of violence, even though Dan apparently imagines it so only to appease Nan, who needs to have patients if she is going to be the town doctor: ". . . accidents will be frequent, owing to wild cattle, fast riding, Indian scrimmages, and the recklessness of a Western life," claims Nan, and Dan obliges by providing a few victims: "I'll scalp a few red fellows or smash up a dozen or so of cowboys for your special benefit" (67–68). Dan's own violence erupts easily when he finds a young victim of card sharps, for he is provoked enough to kill a man in self-defense when he jumps into the game to rescue the young innocent. While trying to be penitent in the penitentiary, Dan is tempted to break out of prison, but a woman "who reminded Dan of Mrs. Jo" (208), probably because Alcott took the incident from her own life, addresses him during a chapel service, and Dan turns away from temptation.

Even after a year in prison Dan is afraid to go home to Plumfield because he still has the look and smell of prison on him. He goes to a mining town where he performs a daring rescue after an accident underground and he is much lionized by the town. But his legs are crushed and he is delirious with pain and fever as a result of his daring, and returns home to Plumfield, splendid for his heroism, but broken in body.

One would think that with all Dan has experienced, he would be thoroughly reformed, enough so that he would be a fit partner in marriage for one of the Plumfield girls. As it turns out, he is in love with Bess, Amy's and Laurie's snow princess; it seems that the situation is ripe for one of Alcott's traditional happy endings. Unfortunately, the elitism that nearly kept Dan out of Plumfield in the first place keeps him out of wedded bliss with one of the March family now, for some sense of Victorian propriety makes the author intervene, and Dan is sent off, with love unrequited, never to marry. As heroic and reformed as he has proven himself, Alcott says that "Few women would care to marry Dan now . . . and it was better to go solitary to his grave" (344).

Dan is the only man in any of Alcott's juvenile books who is single at the end of his story, even though he is the most interesting and most sexual of any of her male characters. To send him out west again as a missionary to the Indians, where he "lived, bravely and usefully . . . till he was shot . . . and at last lay quietly asleep in the green wilderness" (357) would seem to imply that Plumfield and Laurence College cannot bear to have him around, sullying the pristine landscape and feeling his confinement, always ready to break out. The educational methods fall apart here, for Dan is in effect an exile from the paradise of the Marches, be it marriage or home at Plumfield that promises bliss.

Feminism.   The novel's main focus, in spite of its obvious implications for the fruition of Bronson Alcott's educational methods, is women's rights. Josie's and Teddy's fight at the beginning of the book is the opening battle of a war that Alcott wages throughout the novel. In *Jo's Boys* she does not refrain from preaching the feminist gospel, nor does she sugarcoat the sermon's pill by offering her views as simple, good advice. When Stuffy

Cole and Dolly Pettingill, now Harvard students, come home to visit, Mrs. Jo announces, "Yes, I'm going to preach; that's my business, so stand up and take it like men," and reminds them of an earlier conversation when "I was glad to hear you say you would like to have girls at your college; but I hope you will learn to speak more respectfully of them before they come: for that will be the first lesson they will teach you" (265–66). Mrs. Jo and Mrs. Meg conduct a sewing class for the girls at Laurence College. While the girls are learning about tasteful trimmings and styles from Mrs. Amy and the thrifty use of their needles from Mrs. Meg, Mrs. Jo reads to them "copious extracts from Miss Cobbe's 'Duties of Women,' Miss Brackett's 'Education of American Girls,' Mrs. Duffy's 'No Sex in Education,' Mrs. Woolson's 'Dress Reform,' and many of the other excellent books wise women write for their sisters, now that they are waking up and asking, 'What shall we do?'" (276). She reminds the young women that being married is not the only end of life that they may look forward to, and that being a spinster is not the curse it used to be: "Old maids aren't sneered at half as much as they used to be, since some of them have grown famous and proved that woman is n't a half but a whole being, and can stand alone" (277). Alcott may be one of the famous spinsters she has in mind here. Even Mrs. Jo, almost blasphemously, questions whether she should have married; as she looks enviously at Nan's state of single blessedness, she wonders, "I sometimes feel as if I'd missed my vocation and ought to have remained single; but my duty seemed to point this way, and I do n't regret it" (17).

The final triumph of feminism in the book is that the girls are all successful in careers, Nan in medicine, Josie in acting, and Bess in art. Though such careers were not allowed to the March sisters in *Little Women*, all of whom dwindled into wives one way or another in spite of their artistic leanings, the granddaughters are permitted such satisfaction. Perhaps Alcott could afford such frankness about women's rights and such iconoclasm about women's position in society because her royalties were virtually assured with this book. She was a famous author, and any book of hers, especially one about the beloved March family, would sell well. But the new freedom she grants to women here, both in action and in speech, may also be due to an otherwise growing courage on her part to say what she thought, rather than pandering to what her audience wanted her to say.

More likely, however, she felt she could be this frank because in other ways the book is quite conventional about woman's duties to her family. Counterpoised to the spinster Nan is her childhood friend Daisy, a little woman destined to be the happy wife and mother as her mother Meg was in *Little Women*. Josie and Bess do marry, and Mrs. Jo, in spite of her occasional longings for the single life, resolves to be a perfect wife to Professor Bhaer. The joys of career success are undercut by Alcott's description of Mrs. Jo's life as a successful author, even though she is a wife, always hounded by admirers, importuned for money and advice in her voluminous fan mail, and unable to find peace and quiet enough to do the writing she so cherishes. Even more troublesome, her family objects to the time she spends on her writing. If this is success, one could hardly blame a young female reader for not wanting it.

At the end of the book Alcott has tied all the loose strands of the plot together in a big knot, marrying or killing off all her students, as they deserve the one or the other. The fatigue with which she ended the seven-year task of disposing of the March family is evident: with a temperamental outburst Alcott concludes the novel by saying, "It is a strong temptation to the weary historian to close the present tale with an earthquake which should engulf Plumfield and its environs so deeply in the bowels of the earth that no youthful Schliemann could ever find a vestige of it" (357). The March family books show Alcott at her best—a writer of charming stories for children which show them both in happy situations and in problematic ones. Yet even when she appeared to be writing the most conventional domestic and school stories, she maintained at least glimpses of the more complicated aspects of human nature and communal living. Alcott began her career as a writer for children by transforming autobiography into fiction, but she was as true to her real feelings about her family as the limits of fiction for children permitted her to be. The novels may seem preachy and sentimental compared with more modern literature for children, but this perception is due at least partly to changing literary taste and changing social mores. In comparison with her contemporaries, Alcott showed extreme restraint in her didacticism and emotion.

Chapter Three
The Other Juveniles

Alcott's other juvenile novels, five in all, are less well known and less satisfactory in their artistry than are her March family novels, but at the time they were well read, and the better ones still continue to be sold in bookstores and borrowed from libraries. No doubt some of them survive because of the popularity and artistic success of the March stories. As her career as the "children's friend" progressed, Alcott wrote with less imagination than in her earlier works, and she often reworked characters and episodes from the earlier novels into the later novels, sometimes even reworking them to death. She wrote less from her own experiences in these novels and more from invention. When the invention failed, the resulting novels are preachy and dull. Alcott was frequently ill, always busy with causes such as women's suffrage and social welfare movements. Various family members became ill, and her mother and youngest sister died while she was composing some of these novels. Although her outside social activities provided inspiration for her writing, they were nevertheless a drain on her time and energy, and the illnesses and deaths in the family hardly contributed to the creative spirit which sustained her better works. She continued to grind out these novels, as well as short stories, though the effort with which she produced them showed.

But the better novels still retain the best qualities of Alcott's writing for children—warm family life, full characterization, the liveliness of children at play, the details of child life, and local color. Alcott as a well-established writer took more chances, introducing unconventional subjects and characters, and this originality frequently paid off in novels still worthy of attention.

An Old-Fashioned Girl

Between Alcott's two best-known juveniles, *Little Women* (1868–69) and *Little Men* (1871), she wrote *An Old-Fashioned Girl* (1870), a book that is hardly noticed in the Alcott canon. The book was not as commercially successful as either of the March family books, but it did sell well in its own right; twelve thousand copies were sold in advance of the publication date, and Alcott's first royalty check of $6,212 from the book is no small sum even now.[1] The book is about fourteen-year-old Polly Milton, the "old-fashioned girl" of the title, who pays an extended visit to her friend Fanny Shaw of the same age, and the whole Shaw family. The Shaws are wealthy and very new-fashioned in clothing and manners. Yet they are not happy; sixteen-year-old Tom Shaw is left to his own devices; no one in the family takes care of him except his grandmother, who is also ignored by the family. Fanny is lazy and frivolous; Maud, the six-year-old sister, is "fwactious,"[2] as she puts it. Mr. Shaw is totally wrapped up in his business, and his wife is a self-proclaimed invalid, incapable of directing the affairs of her household as she should.

In contrast, the Miltons are as noble as their name. Though the family, much like the Marches, is large and the father a poor country parson, they are as happy as any amount of money might make them. Mrs. Milton, like Marmee, takes an active part in the upbringing of her daughter, advising her by going over the daughter's journal, making comments and answering questions as Abba Alcott did for the young Louisa. She likes to keep Polly plainly and youthfully dressed, for at fourteen Polly is still a girl, even though Fanny Shaw at the same age considers herself a young lady and dresses as much like a grown woman as possible.

Polly also learns "old-fashioned" manners at home—love of family, especially her siblings; respect for her elders; plainness of speech, especially in company; and charity. She is an accomplished needlewoman, capable of turning her gowns and retrimming them to avoid the expense of buying new ones. She is also a good cook. All of these good qualities set her in direct contrast to Fanny Shaw, who, unlike Polly, has never been properly guided in the ways of womanhood. Fanny is concerned only with dressing up, flirting, and gossiping. Even at school she does not apply herself seriously. Of course, Polly is properly horrified at this cavalier attitude toward learning.

Throughout her visit Polly remains true to her "old-fashioned" principles. She shows everyone in the family the proper way to treat each other. She is a companion to the grandmother and gladly listens to the stories of the old woman's girlhood. She pets the older brother and spurs him on to resolution in his studies. She amuses fractious Maud by playing with her and dressing her dolls. Mr. Shaw has her company on his walk to work and his slippers and newspaper from her hands on his arrival home. She runs errands and reads to Mrs. Shaw in her sick room.

Altogether Polly is a regular mother to this family. As Alcott comments, "Mothers do a great deal of this sort of thing, unseen, unthanked, but felt and remembered long afterward, and never lost, for this is the simple magic that binds hearts together, and keeps home happy. Polly learned this secret. She loved to do the 'little things' that others did not see, or were too busy to stop for; and while doing them, without a thought of thanks, she made sunshine for herself as well as others" (53–54).

But lest Polly seem too much like Beth March, an angel in the house too good to last in the real world, Alcott gives her one failing. In spite of what her mother says about the appropriateness of simple dress for young girls, Polly is vain. She wishes she could have fancy clothes like Fanny and her friends. Though she never allows Fanny to dress her up as Meg March does when she visits Vanity Fair, Polly does ask her mother if she may wear jewelry and trim her gown with ruffles and ribbons. Her mother advises her to keep her gown simple, but does send a locket to appease her. Polly wears it like a talisman, for it contains pictures of her parents. So instead of leading her to vanity, it reminds her of her origins and the ways in which her parents would have her act. She does, however, succumb to the temptation of bronze boots. She spends her own money for them, but then suffers pangs of remorse, for she had intended to spend the money on gifts for her family.

Alcott claims that "Polly was by no means a perfect creature" (271). But she only shows her anger when justly provoked, as when the Shaw children read her diary. Polly is in other ways too good to be true. When the Shaws start calling her "sweet P" (138) and "Polly Peacemaker" (122), her function in the novel becomes clear: she is a symbol rather than a flesh-and-blood girl, lacking sufficient human frailty to convince the reader that she is a real girl. Alcott uses Polly, as she says in her preface, "as a possible improvement upon the Girl of the Period, who seems sorrowfully ignorant or ashamed of the good old fashions which make woman truly beautiful and honored, and through her, render home what it should be,—a happy place, where parents and children, brothers and sisters, learn to love and know and help one another" (v–vi).

The contrast between Fanny Shaw, the city mouse, and Polly Milton, the country mouse, is clear; but perhaps it is too clear. Contrasts in real life between characters and situations are never that simple. In any case, at the end of her visit the Shaw family is thoroughly improved and Polly is welcomed back, unsullied by her experiences with the rich and fashionable, by a "group of loving faces at the door of a humble little house, which was more beautiful than any palace in her eyes, for it was home" (141).

The first half of the book is unsatisfying in its simplistic view of the beauty of poverty, simplicity, and "old-fashioned ways." The second part begins with the chapter "Six years Later" and introduces some complexity to the novel. Alcott continued her story at the request of her many readers who demanded a sequel. Polly decided to earn her own living as a music teacher, thereby allowing her family to send her brother Will to college with Polly's share of the household funds. Though Polly goes about her work with a good will, setting up housekeeping on her own, her way is not easy. She wants to break out of her well-regulated ways every once in a while, spending money and having fun in a way that would be truly ruinous to her serious state of mind and her straitened domestic economy. She is not as welcome as she was among Fanny's circle of friends because she is a working woman and not a lady of leisure, and because again she has not the fashionable wardrobe she would need to cut a figure in society.

As a result, Polly frequently feels lonely and deprived. There are times when she despairs: ". . . at the bottom of her heart there was a sore spot still, and the afternoon lessons dragged dismally. It was dusk when she got home, and as she sat in the firelight eating her bread and milk, several tears bedewed the little rolls, and even the home honey had a bitter taste" (169). Her pain sounds like Alcott's own, when she was a young girl just starting out to make her own living; Alcott's sympathy makes Polly's quest to support herself a realistic and sympathetic one.

Fortunately for Polly, she finds a cause to work for. Jane is a poor girl who has attempted suicide because she is ill, has no friends, and cannot find work which would allow her enough to live while still being light enough not to destroy her health. Polly takes Jane's story with her to Fanny's sewing circle. She finds Fanny's fashionable friends shallow in their attitudes toward the poor and charity. As one girl remarks when she is asked to take on some extra sewing for charity, "I think if we meet once a week, it is all that should be expected of us, with our other engagements. Poor people *always* complain that the winter is a hard one, and *never* are satisfied." Another exclaims, "Well, I'm sick of hearing about beggars; I believe half of them are humbugs, and if we let them alone they'd go to work and take care of themselves. There's altogether too much fuss made about charity. I do wish we could be left in peace" (212).

But Polly reveals the girls' own complicity in keeping the poor as they are: "We all complain about bad servants, most as much as if we were house-keepers ourselves; but it never occurs to us to try and mend the

matter, by getting up a better spirit between mistress and maid. . . .
Most of us find money enough for our little vanities and pleasure, but feel
dreadfully poor when we come to pay for work, sewing especially.
Could n't we give up a few of the vanities, and pay the seamstresses better?"
(218). Of course, all the girls resolve to treat their sewing women and
servant girls better, Jane included, and Polly's charitable instincts are
satisfied. She has seen someone whose problems are worse than hers, and,
according to Alcott's formula, she has gotten over her self-pity that way.
Jane also provides Alcott with the opportunity to address the problems of
the working woman, always an important cause for her.

Polly also has love problems, for the second half of the book is devoted
primarily to seeing that Tom, Polly, and Fanny are properly married off to
appropriate partners. The second half opens with Tom engaged to a
woman unworthy of him. She has been engaged several times already, uses
makeup, and has a sharp tongue. Furthermore, she and Tom do not love
each other; Tom offered to marry her simply because he felt sorry for her
after her last engagement was broken. Polly is clearly interested in him,
but of course his prior engagement blocks her maidenly, modest pursuit.
A rich, well-mannered man who appreciates Polly's old-fashioned virtues
is interested in her, but she does not love him, even though she is tempted
to marry him for his money. She suffers as she rejects his suit, for
tender-hearted as she is, she does not wish to hurt his feelings. Fanny is
interested in this man, too, but he is not interested in her because she has
been so spoilt by her contacts with high society.

Both Tom and Fanny are morally improved by a swift reversal of their
father's business affairs. He goes bankrupt, and the family must learn to
take care of itself the way the Milton family has all along. Fanny takes
lessons from Polly on how to keep her wardrobe neat and fashionable
without going to the expense of new gowns. She also learns how to keep
house in her mother's place, for Mrs. Shaw remains an invalid in spite of
the urgent calls of poverty to be up and doing for her family. Soon those
womanly accomplishments make Fanny more attractive to the rich but
old-fashioned gentleman, and by the end of the book he has noted her
improvement and progress. Tom leaves college, where he has been wasting
his father's money anyway, and learns business from his father. He decides
to go into business with one of Polly's brothers in the West and comes back
in a year, more serious and more sure of his love for Polly. Only Maud, the
youngest Shaw, remains single at the end of the book; she "remained a
busy, lively spinster all her days, and kept house for her father in the most

delightful manner" (371). The book ends with a flurry of intended marriages in Alcott's typical happy ending.

However, Alcott offers in this book an alternative to wedded bliss or spinsterhood in the name of filial affection. In the chapter "The Sunny Side" Polly and Fanny visit a women's artist colony. Becky is a sculptress, working on a statue of "the coming woman" who is to be "strong-minded, strong-hearted, strong-souled, and strong-bodied; that is why I made her larger than the miserable, pinched-up woman of our day." Around her feet Becky has placed symbols: "needle, pen, palette, and broom somewhere, to suggest the various talents she owns, and the ballot-box will show that she has earned the right to use them" (258–59). Bess is an engraver; she and Becky live together "Damon and Pythias style. This studio is their home,—they work, eat, sleep, and live here, going halves in everything. They are all alone in the world, but as happy and independent as birds; real friends, whom nothing will part" (255). Kate King, the authoress who "had written a successful book by accident, and happened to be the fashion, just then" (260), drops by for lunch. She is a portrait of Alcott herself when engrossed in the celebrity of *Little Women,* for Kate warns the young women, "My children, beware of popularity; it is a delusion and a snare; it puffeth up the heart of man, and especially of woman; it blindeth the eyes to faults; it exalteth unduly the humble powers of the victim; it is apt to be capricious, and just as one gets to liking the taste of this intoxicating draught, it suddenly faileth, and one is left gasping, like a fish out of water" (262). As Polly looks at her, she notes that "Kate looked sick, tired, and too early old" (263) because of the demands success has placed on her. The five have an impromptu picnic, discussing "their plans, ambitions, successes, and defeats. . . . each cherished a purpose, which seemed to ennoble her womanhood, to give her a certain power, a sustaining satisfaction, a daily stimulus, that led her on to daily effort, and in time to some success in circumstance or character, which was worth all the patience, hope, and labor of her life" (261).

To Fanny, this way of life and dedication to a profession is a revelation: "Men must respect such girls as these . . . yes, and love them too, for in spite of their independence they are womanly. I wish I had a talent to live for, if it would do as much for me as it does for them. . . . Money can't buy these things for me, and I want them very much" (261). She finds there is more to life than the pointless, enervating round of parties and admires the sense of direction that these women have. It is only in one chapter that Alcott posits this alternative to marriage. And even these "strong-minded" women are not immune to the marrying fever that takes over in the second half of the book. Bess is to be married in the spring, and Becky is to remain with her, thereby continuing the bond of friendship in the same degree as before. Although the alternative of satisfying spinsterhood is suggested, it is not taken.

Perhaps Alcott was worried about such a strongly stated feminist ending, especially when she remembered her readers' demands for "Wedding Marches" in the sequel to the first part of *Little Women*. She did not wish to offend her readers or tamper with anything that might affect her royalty statements. She tones down Polly as a feminist mouthpiece: "I want to be strong-minded in the real sense of the word, but I don't like to be called so by people who don't understand my meaning; and I shall be if I try to make the girls think soberly about anything sensible or philanthropic. They call me old-fashioned now, and I'd rather be thought that, though it isn't pleasant, than be set down as a rampant woman's rights reformer" (208). Though Alcott herself was rampant enough, she knew that her public might be offended by strong-mindedness and so took no chances. In fact, none of the writing in *An Old-Fashioned Girl* takes any chances. Alcott simply inverted her formula in *Little Women,* and instead of showing the happiness of poverty, showed the misery of wealth.[3] It is only by making the Shaws poor that she can reform them into the happy family that is characteristic of her juvenile novels.

Eight Cousins

In the time between the writing of *Little Men* and *Eight Cousins* (1875), Louisa Alcott lived the life of a celebrated author. She received many visits and letters from her admiring public and continued to support many social causes which were now glad to have the name of the famous Miss Alcott on their lists of patrons. She also published her adult novel, *Work* (1873).

Alcott's growth as a writer during this time is clear in *Eight Cousins,* the structure of which shows an increasing command of plot. In *Little Men* she was content simply to link together episodic chapters around a common locale and group of characters. In *Eight Cousins* she shows that she can in fact write a novel about a single character; in fact, the plot was so clearly in her mind that her preface to *Eight Cousins* promises a sequel, *Rose in Bloom,* about the same characters in their later years. Though *Eight Cousins* and *Rose in Bloom* still have some of the episodic, short-story quality when the plot turns to the other seven cousins, Rose remains a clear central focus, and it is through her that the coherence of the story is sustained. She is a much more integral part of the plot than the Professor or Mrs. Jo in *Little Men,* either of whom may descend like a *deus ex machina* to resolve conflicts.

Eight Cousins and *Rose in Bloom* present an intensely feminine fictional world. Both novels center around Rose Campbell, an heiress and an orphan, who comes home to her family of aunts and cousins at the age of thirteen, after her father's death. Although she is the ward of her Uncle Alec, her many aunts try to dominate her life and bring her up according to their own peculiar notions about female education. Aunt Clara would send her to a fashionable finishing school; Aunt Myra thinks she is too delicate to live and therefore she should be invalided at home. But Aunt Jane has prevailed and has sent her to a school where she was crammed full of useless intellectual facts, none of which Rose has understood. Aunts Peace and Plenty have tried to amuse and understand Rose, but they cannot understand her ill health and lack of interest in other people. Jessie is the aunt whom Alcott presents as the most understanding. She thinks Rose needs "freedom, rest, and care" and the one thing she cannot have, although her aunts provide themselves as substitutes, is "a Mother."[4] With all these female relations flitting about Rose, each intent on bringing her up in her own way, it is no wonder that the book is subtitled "The Aunt Hill."

Fortunately for Rose and the rest of the story, Uncle Alec arrives to take over his guardianship and to rescue Rose from the nonsensical notions of her many aunts. He takes Aunt Jessie's route with Rose and decides to treat her with "freedom, rest, and care" (40), following some of Bronson Alcott's more conventional yet still unusual advice. He also makes sure Rose stays in contact with her male cousins and encourages them to play together, knowing that Rose will be better for the physical activity and that the boys will be better off for the contact with the refinement of female society, a clear reference to Bronson Alcott's educational theories.

There are seven male Campbell cousins. Charlie, the eldest, is the only son of Aunt Clara, who has spoiled her rich and handsome sixteen-year-old son. Archie, also aged sixteen, is the leader of the group of boys, a steady, reliable boy, brother of Geordie and Will, energetic but otherwise undistinguished eleven- and twelve-year-olds respectively, and Jamie, the baby of the group, who is six. They are all sons of Aunt Jessie, the sensible mother of the book, and are therefore all bound to turn out well. Steve the dandy and Mac the bookworm are about Rose's age, sons of the relentlessly intellectual Aunt Jane. Although Rose is shy with the boys at the beginning, she gradually becomes their chum and confidante.

In spite of the presence of all these boys and the importance of Uncle Alec in Rose's life, the book is filled with feminine details of dressing, manners, and housekeeping. The central theme of the book is woman's education. Even though in her preface Alcott claims that "Uncle Alec's experiment was intended to amuse the young folks, rather than suggest educational improvements for the consideration of the elders," she frequently bogs down into preachiness about what she sees as the evils of the girls' education in its present state. The most memorable topic that Rose studies is dress, for Alcott believes in sensible, though still attractive, clothing for girls. But for someone who claims not to admire the state of female attire at the time, Alcott invests much energy in the details of the fashionable street suit that Rose's aunts choose for her:

The suit was of two peculiar shades of blue, so arranged that patches of light and dark distracted the eye. The upper skirt was tied so tightly back that it was impossible to take a long step, and the under one was so loaded with plaited frills that it "wobbled"—no other word will express it—ungracefully, both fore and aft. A bunch of folds was gathered up just below the waist behind, and a great bow rode a-top. A small jacket of the same material was adorned with a high ruff at the back, and laid well open over the breast, to display some lace and a locket. Heavy fringes, bows, puffs, ruffles, and *revers* finished off the dress, making one's head ache to think of the amount of work wasted, for not a single graceful line struck the eye, and the beauty of the material was quite lost in the profusion of ornament. (204)

Rose is rigged out in a walking suit that makes walking impossible because of the tightness of the gown and the height of the boots. Uncle Alec points out that she will catch cold in such a flimsy fabric, with her throat and head exposed and her feet unprotected against the damp. The crowning indignity of the whole costume is the corset, complete with whalebone stays, that the aunts try to lace Rose into, under the pretext of giving her straightened posture. But Uncle Alec comments that "Nature knows how to mould a woman better than any corset-maker" and threatens to burn the "instrument of torture" (208) except that the whalebones would make a noxious odor.

He offers his alternative suit: pajamas, over which Rose wears "a pretty Gabrielle dress, of a soft, warm shade of brown, coming to the tops of a trim pair of boots with low heels. A seal-skin sack, cap, and mittens, with a glimpse of scarlet at the throat, and the pretty curls tied up with a bright velvet of the same color, completed the external adornment, making her look like a robin redbreast,—wintry, yet warm" (211–12). Aunt Clara is assuaged in that Alec has not dressed the girl in bloomers, the feminist rage at the time; she does admit that the suit is "not unbecoming, if you want her to look like a little schoolgirl; but it has not a particle of style" (211). Of course, when given the choice, Rose chooses Uncle Alec's suit over that of the aunts because it is healthful, comfortable, convenient, and attractive. But Rose, like Alcott as the reader suspects, still admires the fashionable suit and thinks it "pretty" (214).

For all the commonsensical thinking Rose exhibits in this instance, she cannot resist the temptation to have her ears pierced. She knows that her Uncle Alec disapproves, but she cannot resist when a girlfriend offers to "punch" her earlobes. She already has the earrings as part of her inheritance, just waiting in her jewelcase to be worn. The reader finds that Rose's prevailing weakness is vanity, but that Alcott permits this one little indulgence, for Rose is "a girl, after all, and must have her vanities like all the rest of them" (176). Uncle Alec relents and gives her new earrings, pretty gold ones, in spite of his dislike for the whole business. It seems that everyone enjoys Rose for her prettiness, and Alcott will have her even prettier, even if it does feed Rose's vanity and interfere with the moral of the book.

In almost all other matters, however, Uncle Alec prevails. He prescribes fresh air and sunshine, and to see that Rose takes her dose, he gives her a new, breezy, bright bedroom, teaches her to sail, to milk a cow, and to camp. He provides her with gardening tools and, while the two of them lay out the flower beds, teaches her botany. He encourages her to ride a horse, to go skating with the boys, and lets her act like a boy, at least when it comes to physical education. But Uncle Alec considers housework healthy exercise, too, and so when Rose asks him what kind of trade she might take up for her life's work, he suggests "housekeeping" (180) as necessary, healthful, and appropriate. He also urges Rose to learn housewifery, especially cooking and cleaning from her Aunt Plenty, and sewing from her Aunt Peace. He does not consider her education complete until she can produce for him a loaf of brown bread and a shirt with neat buttonholes, those two accomplishments being emblematic of mastery over a number of lesser domestic accomplishments. Alcott, then, proclaims three primary rules in her scheme of woman's education: the necessity of physical education, of traditional female accomplishments about the house, and of mastering some kind of trade, usually a traditional female occupation—for all women, no matter what their financial circumstances. Even though Alcott was a progressive feminist for her time, she still believed that women needed to be skilled in housewifely accomplishments, even if they had careers and the right to vote.

Uncle Alec proposes to take over the supervision of Rose's education for a year as a sort of experiment. If, at the end of that time, anyone in the family objects to Rose's progress, he will relinquish all claims to her guardianship. He first starts by regulating Rose's diet—no more coffee, hot bread, wine, or fried stuff, but only oatmeal, brown bread, fresh milk, and cold water. Bronson Alcott was a vegetarian, a friend of Dr. Graham of Graham Cracker fame, and Isaac Hecker, whose name still adorns a brand of unbleached flour. All his family followed his beliefs, and all supported the temperance movement, although Alcott herself was not above a champagne toast occasionally. The diet Alec prescribes for Rose is certainly a sensible one, with the more eccentric aspects of Bronson's eating habits eliminated. The book also condemns smoking. Although Rose is not tempted, her cousins are, and she talks them into forming an Anti-Tobacco League, much like a Temperance Union, to help them keep their pledge to her not to smoke.

Alec also has a mind to let Rose study more traditional school subjects, although he recognizes that her brains are tired from the cramming of information that went on at the school preferred by Aunt Jane. He teaches her not by having her memorize, but by giving her direct experience. The geography and economy of China are taught by having Rose visit a ship newly arrived with cargo from the Orient. He teaches her arithmetic and keeping of household accounts (again, a part of the household accomplishments that all women should master) by having her keep a record of her expenditures from her allowance. And he teaches her physiology by bringing home an actual skeleton so that she may learn bone structure. In the medical aspect of this last subject Alcott is going beyond traditional school subjects, especially those for girls. She is supporting the education of women physicians, especially in medical schools designed specifically for them, a number of which were founded at the time Alcott was writing.

But in any case, whatever Rose learns she does not learn from books. Alec allows her to study only when she begs him to, so that she may teach what she learns to a servant girl. This avoidance of books does not imply that Alcott would not have girls read, or that she does not respect good books, for the most admirable men in *Eight Cousins* are the learned Uncle Alec and her bookworm cousin Mac. But Mac is an object lesson in what happens when children devote themselves too much to books. He endangers his sight from reading too much in the sun at a time when other children are playing, and his road to recovery is a long, difficult one. If children read, says Alcott, they should do so in moderation.

While Mac is recovering, Rose reads to him more good books, "travels, biographies, and the history of great inventions or discoveries" (120), even though he would rather study Greek and Latin. But he does not resort to the adventure novels that his cousins Will and Geordie read, which Alcott attacks with a vengence. She calls them "*optical* delusions," a reference to the Oliver Optic books of William T. Adams, of a rival publishing company, Lee and Shepard. Alcott, through the character of Aunt Jessie, criticizes the books for having bad grammar, a criticism which she often heard about her own books. The boys counter that such language makes the books realistic, especially if the characters are uneducated, but Aunt Jessie answers, "my sons are neither boot-blacks nor newsboys, and I object to hearing them use such words as 'screamer,' 'bully,' and 'buster.'" In fact, she points out, the books are not realistic at all: "Now, I put it to you, boys, is it natural for lads from fifteen to eighteen to command ships, defeat pirates, outwit smugglers, and so cover themselves with glory, that Admiral Farragut invites them to dinner, saying: 'Noble boy, you are an honor to your country!'" (196). It is difficult to understand exactly why Alcott decided to attack these books, especially the Oliver Optic series. Perhaps she was attacking a successful series by a rival publisher; perhaps she was trying to sell her own book and her others like it. Perhaps the criticism was sour grapes; she sometimes felt that her books for children were "moral pap," and she did not dare risk her profits by writing more adventurous stories as she might have liked. It is clear from her adult thrillers that she was capable of writing stories of improbable, even immoral, high adventure. It may be that she attacked the Oliver Optic books to justify to herself and to the public the kind of novel for children she did write, even while she longed to write in the "optical style" herself.

This is one of the few times in the novel that Alcott talks about her curriculum for educating boys; but she had already examined that topic at length in *Little Men,* so perhaps she had nothing else to say on that matter. The Campbell boys are educated in the novel through the agency of Rose. She learns that her vocation in life will be to reform the world of men by exerting her "influence" and being charitable to the less fortunate. Rose, therefore, must give up her dearly loved earrings as part of a bargain to get her cousins not to smoke. She stays at her cousins' houses for a month at a time, even though she would rather not, to influence them to be mannerly and to stay away from the vices that tempt young men who may fall in with the wrong kind of company. As she says to Uncle Alec, "I have discovered what girls are made for . . . To take care of boys" (280). As independent and strong-minded as Alcott would like women to be, she still finds that they are the moral guardians of the world, standing high on the pedestal where Victorian men had placed them, and caring for men who are obviously unable to take care of themselves.

Rose takes on her traditional Victorian role as Lady Bountiful when she decides to adopt Phebe, a servant girl, as her sister. Phebe has talent as a singer, although it is uncultivated because of her position. When Rose first meets her, Phebe points out how lucky the young heiress is: "I'm sure you ain't all alone with such a lot of folks belonging to you, and all so rich and clever . . . I'm sure I should think I was in clover if I had folks and money, and nothing to do but enjoy myself" (7–8). Phebe envies Rose not only for her life of leisure but also for her education; Phebe is trying to teach herself to read and write using the old recipes she finds in the kitchen and a makeshift copybook. Rose decides to "adopt" Phebe, since she is an orphan, and Uncle Alec readily consents to become Phebe's guardian. Rose helps Phebe learn to read and write; she offers to give Phebe some of her clothes. Even though the modern reader may find Rose's generosity patronizing, Phebe does not: "As for patronizing, you may walk on me if you want to, I won't mind" (57). Rose sees her role as "a fairy godmother" (58) to Phebe. But at least she does so with Aunt Peace's words in mind, "in one sense we are all sisters, and should help one another" (56). Phebe never really does become a full-fledged sister in the Campbell clan, although she is later a sister-in-law, but Rose is following Alcott's rather revolutionary (at least for the time) idea about charity, that the deserving poor need, not a handout, but the means to help themselves.

Eight Cousins as a whole has much charm to it, though the characters are not all as well imagined as they were in *Little Women.* As in *Little Men,* the boys each seem to have one main characteristic, though Alcott's writing is particularly strong in characterizing Uncle Alec, Mac, and Charlie. Rose, like Polly Milton in *An Old-Fashioned Girl,* tends to be too much of a symbol, as "a rose among thorns" and other such wordplays indicate; but she is rescued from plaster sainthood by her vanity and playfulness. The book is certainly an issue-oriented one, concerned with using characters as occasions for discussing various educational ideas. In spite of these objections, there is a warmth to the clan, a spontaneity about the children, and a sense of humor about the foibles of the adults, that help the book to succeed in spite of its ideological bent.

Rose in Bloom

Alcott wrote *Rose in Bloom* about a year after *Eight Cousins.* In that year she attended the Women's Congress, a suffragist conference in Syracuse, and spent much of the winter on holiday in New York. While in New York, she visited the Tombs prison, the Randall's Island orphanage and home for retarded and handicapped children, and the Newsboys Lodging House. Many of Alcott's activities in this intervening period appear, somewhat transformed, in *Rose in Bloom*.

The book opens about seven years after the close of *Eight Cousins;* Rose and Phebe have spent a few years in Europe, Rose being "finished" in her education with the Grand Tour, while Phebe has studied music. During that time Uncle Alec has taught Rose to be even more "strong-minded" than before, and decidedly "odd,"[5] as her friends put it. In fact, as soon as she gets home, her feminist thinking is clearly and strongly expressed, with a degree of bitterness not typical of Rose elsewhere. Charlie suggests that her chief occupation now that she is home will be to become an ornament to society until she marries. Rose has other ideas:

. . . I believe that it is as much a right and a duty for women to do something with their lives as for men; and we are not going to be satisfied with such frivolous parts. . . . Would *you* be contented to be told to enjoy yourself for a little while, then marry and do nothing more till you die? We've got minds and souls as well as hearts; ambition and talents, as well as beauty and accomplishments; and we want to live and learn as well as love and be loved. I'm sick of being told that is all a woman is fit for! I won't have any thing to do with love till I prove that I am something beside a housekeeper and a baby-tender!

Charlie's comment after being so thoroughly rebuffed is, "Heaven preserve us! here's women's rights with a vengeance!" (10–11).

The reader may wonder quite legitimately if Alcott is getting a bit carried away with the feminism here. Rose has not really experienced enough of life to be so vehement in her feelings about the way men have confined women's activities. Hers has been a rather privileged position, for her money and social class have permitted her to act as she wished, without regard to social mores. The voice in these two passages is clearly Alcott's. Though in her preface she issues the disclaimer that "there is no moral to this story," such preachy rhetoric does not reassure the reader.

Rose continues to be strong-minded, but she does not seem to be nearly as morally straightlaced as she is in the opening of the book. After returning from Europe she decides that the first activity she would like to pursue is three months of high society, going to balls and dinners, dressing up in elegant gowns, staying up late, and otherwise being as thoroughly frivolous as society permits a young heiress to be. Uncle Alec has taught her to be more noble in her leisure pursuits than this, and Rose admits that she knows better, but just cannot resist: "I know it is foolish; but I do want to be a regular butterfly for a little while and see what it is like. You know I could n't help seeing a good deal of fashionable life abroad, though we were not in it; and here at home the girls tell me about all sorts of pleasant things that are to happen this winter; so, if you won't despise me *very* much, I should like to try it" (50). Although Uncle Alec may look very sorely troubled by Rose's decision, the reader does not condemn her so strongly, for she does have a pleasant time in society which makes for interesting reading. Instead, the reader is likely to excuse Rose as one of her uncles does: "train a girl as wisely as you choose, she will break loose when the time comes, and go in for pleasure as eagerly as the most frivolous, for ''tis in their nature to'" (53).

Rose finds that all is not as pleasant as it seems to be, for her new friends have ulterior motives; "half the people who are so kind to me don't care a bit for me, but for what I can give them; and that makes me unhappy, because I was so glad and proud to be liked" (64). The young men who have posed themselves as suitors have been even more exasperating: "I was not prepared to have men propose at all times and places, with no warning but a few smiles and soft speeches. . . . One absurd boy proposed when we'd only met half a dozen times. But he was dreadfully in debt, so that accounted for it perhaps" (70). Rose has led a rather sheltered life and is surprised not to find in the glittering world of society the gold that she had expected.

Uncle Alec's strong-minded upbringing prevails, for after three months, Rose decides to give up society, not because she wants to, but more because she finds it seductive and unhealthful. This is a rather doubtful victory for Uncle Alec, since Rose quits society for insufficient reasons; it is not as distasteful to her as Uncle Alec thinks it should be. Rose, like the reader and Alcott, has enjoyed herself at Vanity Fair, thereby somewhat compromising Alcott's moral in favor of humanizing her character and entertaining her reader.

In any case, Rose sets about on another plan; she has decided to take up philanthropy as her vocation. During her trip to Europe she says that Uncle Alec "was interested in hospitals and prisons, and I sometimes went with him: but they made me sad; so he suggested other charities, that I could help about when we came home. I visited Infant Schools, Working-women's Homes, Orphan Asylums, and places of that sort. You don't know how much good it did me, and how glad I am that I have the means of lightening a little some of the misery in the world" (82–83). Rose has toured various charitable agencies in Europe much as Alcott did during her trip to New York. As a result of her shopping around for a

cause, she has decided to convert two of her inherited houses in the city
into rooming houses, "comfortable homes for poor but respectable women
to live in. There is a class who cannot afford to pay much, yet suffer a great
deal from being obliged to stay in noisy, dirty, crowded places like
tenement-houses and cheap lodgings. I can help a few of them, and I'm
going to try." Again Rose applied Alcott's principle that the poor should
not receive handouts but rather the means by which to rehabilitate
themselves: "uncle showed me that it was wiser not make genteel paupers
of them, but let them pay a small rent and feel independent. I don't want
the money of course, and shall use it in keeping the houses tidy, or helping
other women in like case" (84). Rose finds this sort of charity difficult, for
later the homes run into problems: "Rose was disturbed to find that the
good people expected her to take care of them in a way she had not
bargained for. . . . Things were neglected, water-pipes froze and burst,
drains got out of order, yards were in a mess, and rents behindhand" (256).
She continues her project, but leaves it in the hands of a manager and turns
her interest to orphans.

   She adopts one of them from a workhouse, a hopeless case brought home
to her by her cousin Mac. Dulcinea, or Dulce, as she is named (since Mac is
her Don Quixote), is Rose's surrogate child, on whom Rose gets to try out
her abilities as a baby-tender. Though she never quite rescues and rehabili-
tates Dulce the way she rescues Phebe, by making a huge social success out
of her, the baby does give Mac ideas about a homey family grouping,
including himself, Rose, and Dulce: "Mac could not help thinking that
they looked a little like the Flight into Egypt," with Rose looking like one
of "Correggio's young Madonnas" (263). The reader can perceive readily
which cousin Rose will finally marry.

   But, at least in the beginning of the book it appears that Rose will
marry Charlie, the "Prince," as his cousins call him. Charlie's difficulty as
a likely suitor is that he has no vocation, no work at hand to take up in
order to give his life purpose. Rose spots his dissolution as soon as she steps
off the ship at the beginning of the book: "something was amiss with
Charlie" (3). She tries to rouse him from his languor, to stir him up
through love of her. At first he argues that his function in the family is
purely decorative: "There always ought to be one gentleman in the family,
and that seems to be rather my line" (3). Being the ornament to society
that he is, he has been unduly influenced by his social companions, most of
whom have had a bad influence on him, for he has taken to drinking, his
ultimate downfall. Rose again binds him to a promise not to drink, and
finally convinces him to go to his father in India and become part of the

family importing business. But before he leaves, Charlie takes one fatal last drink of champagne, which is his literal downfall; in his drunkenness he neglects to control his high-spirited horse, is thrown, and dies from internal injuries.

Charlie's drink is the most reprehensible act that any of Alcott's fictional children ever commit, especially since Charlie had made his pledge of temperance to Rose. A woman's "influence" was considered sacred at that time; the idea was that a woman would exert her power not by action, but by example, living herself a life beyond reproach and leading her menfolk in the ways of righteousness by the light of her halo.[6] When she exacted a promise from one of her men, it had the power of a solemn vow, and to have broken the vow was to offend the sanctity of the woman's saintliness. Charlie in that one drink made himself permanently unworthy. Alcott's good women, indeed almost all good women in Victorian fiction, had this power. Rose is one of Alcott's most accomplished practitioners in the art of influence; in *Eight Cousins* she teaches all of her cousins good manners, good morals, and social graces simply by her pure and radiant presence. The only stain on her soul is her vanity, but even that she gives up most willingly "to influence" her boys, as when she sacrifices her earrings to get them to give up cigars.

All the boys fall in line except Charlie. He is the only serious challenge to the doctrine of "influence" in the two books; his death shows that the presence of a good woman cannot by itself reform a man. Charlie has been under the indulgent, misguided "influence" of his mother, Aunt Clara, for too long to be rescued, even by Rose. Uncle Alec exclaims that Clara has permanently damaged him: "I can hardly blame him for what he is, because his mother did the harm. . . . I sometimes feel as if I must break out against that woman, and thunder in her ears that she is ruining the immortal soul for which she is responsible to heaven" (166). Clara's influence has been decidedly bad; the only way to salvation for Charlie lies in the path to India, but he does not leave in time to escape the final temptation offered by the fatal glass of champagne. The death sentence seems particularly harsh to the modern reader; after all, Charlie is not bad, only misguided. His death is a measure of the urge to preach that Alcott felt in this book; when she finds a wayward and unreformed sinner who cannot easily be saved, she can find no other way to deal with him than to kill him off.

The harshness of Charlie's treatment can also be explained by the two themes of the book: finding one's vocation and one's true love. All of the other young men in the book, and Rose herself, find something to do to keep them occupied and away from the temptations of drink to which Charlie succumbs. All find vocations that improve not only the world around them but themselves. Archie becomes an earnest businessman and proves by his seriousness and stability that his love for Phebe is real; Phebe earns fame and fortune as a singer and yet continues to love Archie, thereby proving that she does not love him only for his money. Kitty Van Tassel is a flighty girl, but following Rose's example learns steadiness, housewifeliness, and charity; she makes a suitable wife for Steve, who accepts her influence. Even the boys at school, Will, Geordie, and Jamie, keep their wits about them, though they might just as easily take up dissipation as other young college men do.

And then there is Mac. Rose begins her campaign of "influence" upon him in *Eight Cousins,* when she nurses him through his long difficulty with his eyesight and teaches him not to rant and rage at his fate, but to bear it calmly and wait for time to heal him. She studies physiology with him under Uncle Alec's tutelage. While she is away in Europe, Mac has graduated from college. But though she sees that he is much improved when she arrives home, he is not yet the perfect partner for her. First she must get through all the business with Charlie, and then she must see to Mac's manners in society. At the beginning of the book he shows that he has the will to apply himself to the vocation of medicine, making him as worthy of her love as Uncle Alec, the other physician in the book. But he is an embarrassment at parties and balls, and Rose as an heiress will need a partner who can cut a good figure in society with her. Accordingly, he learns to dance, dress appropriately, and to tend to his partner as a gentleman should, rather than leaving her to her own devices at parties.

But even this is not enough for Rose; Mac must take himself away from her presence and prove his love. Rose has high hopes for him: "you must be famous. . . . I'm very ambitious for you; because, I insist upon it, you are a genius of some sort" (272). He therefore leaves her, earns his physician's diploma, and publishes a book of poetry which makes him famous in fashionable society, where he remembers his manners and acquits himself admirably. Rose expects much of the man she will marry: "love is n't all. I must look up, not down, trust and honor with my whole heart, and find strength and integrity to lean on" (292). But Mac has already gained her respect, as she freely admits, and he sets about to earn the rest, to be as much as possible like Uncle Alec, the man she loves, trusts, honors, respects, and depends on already.

In the end Mac finally wins her, but not until Alcott turns him into a character as much like a renaissance man as possible. He is already a poet and a physician, an unlikely combination. He also takes up geology and botany and other hobbies, spending his vacations camping in the mountains by himself and reappearing sunburnt, with a "sylvan freshness [and] . . . reposeful strength" (271) about him, shaggy hair, beard and all. On his vacations he reads Keats and Emerson and especially Thoreau, for as he says, "A fellow can't spend 'A Week' with Thoreau and not be the better for it. . . . even an hour with such a sane, simple, and sagacious soul as his must help one" (276). When asked whether he ever gets lonely on his solitary rambles, he replies, "'Never: I take my best friends along, you know,' and he gave a slap to the pocket from which peeped the volume of Thoreau" (283). He turns out to be an exceptional, though somewhat improbable young man, especially given his earlier antisocial predilections as a bookworm. When he gives Rose a statue of Cupid to accompany the one of Psyche on her mantelpiece, it becomes clear how idealistic Alcott envisions their union to be, the archetypal true love match.

The book finishes with much pairing off: Rose with Mac, Steve with Kitty Van Tassel, and Archie with Phebe, in spite of all the protestations of strong-minded feminism at the beginning of the book. Of all these pairs, Archie and Phebe have the most trouble because of the inequality of their respective social positions. Archie falls in love with Phebe at first sight, and Phebe reciprocates soon after. In spite of the fact that Rose is all for the match, the rest of the family, including the otherwise open-minded Uncle Alec, opposes it. Rose may have accepted Phebe as her sister, but no one else sees her as a social equal. Even Phebe sees the family's point and removes herself to a distant city to prove her ability to take care of herself. After a year of testing, in which Phebe distinguishes herself as a teacher of music and a chorister in one of the more prestigious churches in a large city, the two are reunited, this time with the family's blessing.

The whole business reeks of a class-conscious snobbery that is unexpected, given Alcott's rather progressive views on education and women's rights. The same snobbery shows up again in *Jo's Boys,* with the March family's objections to the possible love matches of Daisy and Bess to Nat and Dan, the poor boys of the story. It is difficult to know whether the issue was simply one of Alcott's blind spots or whether she thought that her readers would not accept Phebe's work-callused hands touching those of the well-born, privileged Campbell boys without proving her worthiness.

Under the Lilacs

Under the Lilacs (1878) is Alcott's blandest juvenile novel. It is the story of Bab and Bess Moss, eight- and nine-year-old girls, who are joined in their home by a runaway from a circus, fourteen-year-old Ben Brown and his show dog Sancho. Although there is no direct evidence that James Otis, author of *Toby Tyler, or Ten Weeks with a Circus* (1881), knew Alcott's work, the proximity of the books' publication dates suggests that if Otis had not read the book, he may have known of it; or perhaps he was simply responding, like Alcott, to the popular appetite for circus stories.

As in *Jack and Jill,* the best scenes are those that show the children playing together, putting on dramatic presentations, having parties with dolls, or speaking their pieces at class day. Again, the reader suspects that these scenes were drawn from real life, and the details that Alcott observed at the original events make the fictional representations much more convincing. Otherwise, the book is quite strained in its creation of characters and plot.

The most interesting characters are Ben and his pet dog. Ben, after he has been cleaned up, dressed, and fed by Bab's and Bess's mother, still retains the sparkling quality that must have made him a circus success as "Master Adolphus Bloomsbury, after I stopped bein' a flyin' Coopid and a Infant Progidy."[7] He has plenty of self-confidence and energy, and moves gracefully and readily to do any task at hand. He has wonderful stories to tell about the circus and gains much pity when he tells of the abuse he suffered at the hands of his master. He wants to become "respectable" (97); the problem with him as a character is that he becomes too respectable too quickly. He has only to pass a school in order to remind himself of his ignorance and to devise a remedial plan of study. The rich young lady next door admonishes him gently about his cursing, and he immediately gives it up. She takes him to church with her, and he immediately gets religion. The home influences that this young lady exerts are too easily accepted, both by Ben and by Alcott, as reforming graces.

The only snag in Ben's rapid rise to respectability is an incident in which he is accused of stealing money from the young lady. Both she and her younger brother indict him, excusing any of the other servants around the house on the grounds that they are perfectly trustworthy. Like Nat Blake in *Little Men,* Ben is presumed guilty of theft because of circumstantial evidence until happenstance clears him. Unlike Nat, Ben does not have a history of deceit. It is difficult to feel kindly toward the young lady after

her unfair suspicions. It may only be that Alcott took an old motif from
Little Men and applied it with little alteration or thought to *Under the
Lilacs,* failing to notice that it may have worked well in the former but that
circumstances were different in the latter.

The little dog Sancho is appealing simply because pets in general are
attractive and because this dog is clever. Twice he is separated from Ben,
and twice he travels long distances to rejoin his master. He also does tricks
such as spelling his name with blocks and dancing on his hind legs. He is
also used as an instrument for punishing Ben when he strays too far from
the locus of respectability, the young lady and her house. Ben goes to the
circus without permission and is momentarily tempted to rejoin his old
way of life. In a moment of inattentiveness Sancho is stolen away, and Ben
is left without his closest friend in the world. Later in the story Ben is told
that his father, whom he expected to return to care for his son, from a trip to
the West, is dead. It is hard enough that the boy should find himself
orphaned; to have lost his dog, too, and for such a pitifully minor
infraction as going to the circus without permission, an excusable temptation for a young boy, seems doubly unfair. It is right after the news of his
father's death that he is accused of stealing. Alcott is not dealing with a
wild firebrand in Ben as she was with Dan Kean in *Little Men* and *Jo's Boys.*
Yet she seems to be punishing him with circumstances extreme enough for
a boy of Dan's intractability.

The story has a happy ending, for Sancho escapes and returns to Ben,
minus his tail, as a reminder to Ben of the suffering the dog has undergone
as a result of his misdemeanor. The young lady atones for her suspicions of
Ben's honesty by giving him an extravagant birthday party and by
suggesting that his friend Bab should let him win an archery contest, even
though she is as good a shot as he is. Alcott seems entirely too willing here
to compromise her feminist principles; in another novel Bab would have
stood her ground. Ben's father returns to him, having been extremely ill
although not quite dead, and therefore *incommunicado.* And finally, Ben's
father and Mrs. Moss, the girls' mother, marry, thereby guaranteeing that
Ben will never have to leave home and its good influences again. Of course,
he also will not ever experience the excitement of his past again either. But
in this rather simplistic book the reader is supposed to accept that home is
the highest value there is.

Alcott was much preoccupied at the time by her mother's illness, and
Mary Mapes Dodge, editor of *St. Nicholas,* had some trouble getting her to
finish the novel so that it could be published in that magazine. By 1877
Alcott could publish almost anything, and her public would read it

enthusiastically. Perhaps she was tired and worried, perhaps just interested in making enough money to care for her mother in her last days. In any case, the lack of invention and interest on Alcott's part is all too evident in the novel.

Jack and Jill

Alcott first published *Jack and Jill* in serialized form in Mary Mapes Dodge's *St. Nicholas* magazine in 1879 and 1880. It may be that the book's manner of publication influenced its composition, for it is episodic, each chapter concentrating on one character or one small group of characters. But Alcott used the same compositional method in *Little Women* and *Little Men,* and to some extent in *Eight Cousins* and *Rose in Bloom. Jack and Jill* is a "village story" as Alcott says in her dedication; the story takes place in Harmony Village, Alcott's transformation of her hometown of Concord. There is a whole flock of young people in the story, as there was in Concord at the time. But the story concentrates on three girls, Merry Grant, Molly Bemis, and Jane Pecq, the "Jill" of the story, and three boys, Jack and Frank Minot, modeled after Alcott's nephews John and Fred Pratt (the name Minot was one of their father's family names) and Ed Devlin, transformed from Ellsworth Devens, whose death inspired Alcott to write the book.

The story takes place over the course of nearly a year. It opens with a nasty sliding accident which nearly kills Jack and Jill, and shows their recovery, both physical and moral, throughout the year. The other children are sobered and inspired to do better by the near tragedy that befalls Jack and Jill, and also undertake to improve. While individual chapters are devoted to the moral progress of individual characters, in several interludes they are all brought together for celebrations that must have been inspired by actual events in the lives of the young people at Concord; a Christmas party, a dramatic production in honor of Washington's Birthday, the May Day celebration with flowers and baskets, a weekend at a shore resort, a school exhibition that was certainly inspired by Bronson Alcott's class recitation days when he was superintendent of the Concord public schools, and Ed Devlin's funeral.

Ellsworth Devens, Ed's real-life counterpart, may have been an exceptionally good boy, but if he had the very human faults that might be expected in even a well-behaved young man, Alcott does not let them into the picture she creates as a memorial to him. As he appears in *Jack and Jill,* Ed is a saint, destined from the first to be too good for life. He is "the one big boy who never was rough with the small ones."[8] As one would expect, his physical appearance and manners are attractive: "a sweet-faced lad, with a laugh on his lips, a fine color on his brown cheek, and a gay word for every girl he passed" (2). He drops out of school before graduating, leaving behind all the fun that his friends are having, to go into business in order to support his mother. The one characteristic that relieves this unrelenting portrait of sweetness and light is "a gay word for every girl he passed"; indeed, some of his gestures are grandiloquent: "Ed, the gentle squire of dames, spreading his overcoat on the sled as eagerly as ever Raleigh laid down his velvet cloak for a queen to walk upon" (2). There is a subdued smile on everyone's face when he argues at a boys' debating society meeting the question, "Shall girls go to college with us?" for as he says, "I think that school would be awfully dry and dismal without—ahem!—any young ladies to make it nice" (115). He is a constant comfort to Jack during his recovery, and a gallant admirer of Jill.

Ed does not take as long to die of his mysterious "fever" as does Beth March, just a week, which takes up only part of the chapter about his death and funeral. There is no deathbed scene, but all the children attend his funeral. Apparently the taste for sentimental deaths in children's literature had changed, for Alcott intrudes in the narrative to defend her inclusion of Ed's death:

It is often said that there should be no death or grief in children's stories. It is not wise to dwell on the dark and sad side of these things; but they have also a bright and lovely side, and since even the youngest, dearest, and most guarded child cannot escape some knowledge of the great mystery, is it not well to teach them in simple, cheerful ways that affection sweetens sorrow, and a lovely life can make death beautiful? I think so . . . (267–68).

The children decorate the church where the funeral is held, hear the eulogy, and see the interment. They are, of course, inspired to follow Ed's example, so that they too can be so admired when they come to be eulogized, for they realize that "it was not what he did but what he was that made him so beloved. All that was sweet and noble in him still lives; for goodness is the only thing we can take with us when we die, the only thing that can comfort those we leave behind, and help us to meet again hereafter" (269–70). The chapter closes with the tearful rendition of Ed's favorite hymn.

In the last chapter Jack and Frank Minot each take an acorn from the tree growing over Ed's grave and plant them to remind them of him and to inspire them: "the planting of the acorns was a symbol of the desire budding in those young hearts to be what he might have been, and to make their lives nobler for the knowledge and love of him" (333). The portrait of Ed is certainly a sentimentalized one, and although she avoids the emotional outbursts that might have taken place had Ed's deathbed been described, Alcott gives those emotions full play at the funeral. She is capable of creating imperfect yet still good and lovable children; a little more of such realism in devising her memorial to Ed Devlin-Ellsworth Devens would have avoided many of the emotional excesses and would have created just as appealing a portrait.

The book's main theme is that children's upbringing should provide them with "good health, good principles, and a good education" (306). As an educational novel, *Jack and Jill* reworks many of the themes found in earlier Alcott novels. The boys' debating society considers the issue of coeducation, as mentioned above; the boys in the book all join the Lodge and take a pledge not to drink; the girls form their own club and decide to take up "missionarying" (41), that is, reforming some specific part of their lives, by using their female "influence." The girls think that they would like to go to some place exotic to do their reforming, but Mrs. Pecq, Jill's mother, points out that there is much work for all of them to do at home.

Jill, a "wild . . . little savage," decides to "make a pretty-mannered lady" (41) of herself. Merry Grant's task is to help her mother and set "the big brothers a good example" by making "plain things nice and comfortable, and not long[ing] for castles before she knows how to do her own tasks well" (41). By her example and "influence," her brothers, all hulking farmboys, learn to appreciate beauty and refinement; and Merry herself learns the pleasure of serving and satisfying her menfolk. Molly Bemis undertakes to civilize her heathenish little brother, attending to his and her own cleanliness and appearances, thereby "influencing" her widowed father to take more interest in his home and his children. All the little missionaries succeed, but not without some setbacks. Still, the doctrine of female influence overcomes all, as it usually does in Alcott's novels, and improves not only the girls, but also the boys.

But the reform of the children, most especially Jack and Jill, is a particularly violent one. Jill, in her willfulness, precipitates the accident that sets the story going because she takes a dare from a boy: "Joe said I wouldn't dare to do it, so I must" (5). The sled run that Jack and Jill take is a dangerous one, and to compound the danger, "Jill forgot to hold tight and Jack to steer carefully." At the point of the accident Alcott moralistically intrudes: "oh, alas, for Jack and Jill, who wilfully chose the wrong road and ended their fun for the winter!" (7). Jack breaks a leg, which slows him down for a month or two, but he goes back to school, while Jill is left to recover from a back injury that might have crippled her for life and that forces her to be still for several months. As soon as the accident happens, Jill is filled with self-destructive remorse: "I want to be cold and ache and have horrid things done to me. Oh, if I ever get out of this bed I'll be the best girl in the world, to pay for this" (14). She does in fact spend nearly the rest of the book aching and having horrid things done to her to pay for her one moment of willfulness, in which she sounds peculiarly like Alcott's feminist characters: "You boys think girls like mean little coasts without any fun or danger in them, as if we couldn't be brave and strong as well as you" (7). But Jill is not allowed her moment of independence and equality with the boys. Alcott finds that the way to tame such high spirits is to keep the girl flat on her back until she learns better.

The example set for her to follow is a modern-day St. Lucy who is known in the neighborhood. As an invalid, this Lucy "was so patient, other people were ashamed to complain of their small worries; so cheerful, that her own great one grew lighter; so industrious, that she made both money and friends by pretty things she worked and sold to her many visitors. And best of all, so wise and sweet that she seemed to get good out of everything, and make her poor room a sort of chapel where people went for comfort, counsel and an example of pious life. So, you see, Lucinda was not so very miserable after all" (85).

In effect, Jill is offered the position of plaster saint in her own chapel of a home. It takes a good deal of reforming to make the "little gypsy of a girl, with . . . a face full of fun and sparkle" (3) into St. Lucy, as it did to make Jo March over into a Marmee or a Beth. Alcott resorts to physical crippling in this case. After her transformation, Jill receives the same rewards as Jo: a loving husband, this time in the person of Jack. Although Alcott does allow Molly Bemis to remain single, even she becomes a household saint: "Molly remained a merry spinster all her days, one of the independent, brave and busy creatures of whom there is such need in the world to help take care of other peoples' wives and children, and do the many useful jobs that the married folk have no time for" (323). This may have been the kind of ending that Alcott's readers wanted; or perhaps the book ends this way because Alcott had not the artistic vision that might beatify, but at the same time immobilize, her character.

The schooling that goes on in the book sounds remarkably like Bronson Alcott's. When Jack brings home a report from the schoolmaster with a less-than-perfect mark for behavior, he is ashamed to show it to his mother because "she cared more for good behavior than for perfect lessons" (174), as Bronson Alcott did. She also thinks that "boys make better men for learning to use the talents they possess . . . as . . . tools with which to carve their own fortunes." Each boy should learn a trade; "and the best help toward this end is an example of faithful work, high aims, and honest living" (47), so Mrs. Minot surrounds her sons with exemplary young men, including Ed Devlin. She distinctly deemphasizes book learning and reemphasizes good living; therein lies her support for temperance and for coeducation and the good "influence" that girls exert on boys. She finally takes her sons out of school so that their bodies and minds can develop in fresh air and worldly experience. It is she who proposes the educational fair so that all the children have the opportunity to show their expertise at matters other than scholarship. Though she does not have a conscience book like Mrs. Jo in *Little Men,* Mrs. Minot does sound like Mrs. Jo, transported from Plumfield to Harmony Village.

In *Jack and Jill* Alcott takes no chances with her formulae for success—a good child dying, girls and boys helping each other to be good, educational methods that deemphasize traditional intellectual pursuits, advocacy of temperance, moderate feminism coupled with the doctrine of women's influence, and marriage at the end. The most interesting scenes are the children's celebrations of various holidays, where Alcott's reporter's eye brings to the narrative humorous details that make the festivals and youthful high spirits particularly charming. But the treatment of Jill, the activities of the "missionarying" girls, and Ed Devlin's death and funeral are formulae that have gone flat from Alcott's continual use of them and her increasing sentimentalism. The spirits of the children get them into trouble sometimes—Frank Minot nearly burns down the house, and Molly Bemis's younger brother gives everyone food poisoning by letting them eat his pet lobster, dead and decayed. But these subversive passages where the children nearly destroy those things that the reader holds dear are not as frequent or as suggestive as they were in *Little Women* or *Little Men.*

Critical Reputation

Of these five novels, *Eight Cousins* and *Rose in Bloom* are the best known, and most successful. The popularity of the one trades on the other, since the latter is the sequel to the former. But the two succeed on the strength of the first, with its clear portrayal of children at their games and its

presentation, in utter rationality, of Alcott's somewhat unusual ideals
about woman's education. Rose marries, as a good comic heroine should,
but her path to marriage is not easy, and her resolve to have a career does
not fit easily either with her desire for social intercourse or with her role as
an heiress. Though Alcott is sometimes preachy in her harangues about
women's rights, to hear such views voiced so clearly is original and
interesting in a children's novel, even now. *An Old-Fashioned Girl, Jack and
Jill,* and *Under the Lilacs* suffer in comparison with the other two novels
because in them Alcott simply reworks characters and situations that had
succeeded in other novels, and instead of investing her energies in original
ideas, channels her verve into sermonizing.

Chapter Four
Works for Adults

Though she was popularly known as the "children's friend," Louisa May Alcott began her career, and most enjoyed, writing for adults. It was only when she was writing for adults that she reported being caught up in a "vortex" of creativity and enthusiasm about her work; her juvenile novels were produced laboriously. *Little Women* was not particularly tedious for her, but the composition of her other juveniles was frequently managed only by sticking to a rigid schedule which insured a daily quota of pages produced. The reader of her diaries and her public proclamations about her lack of interest in writing for children may suspect that she was not entirely fair about her works for children and her interest in them; they did, after all, make her reputation, insure a ready market for reprints of her earlier adult novels, and provide her with financial security. Perhaps some of her disdain is the result of the low esteem in which children's writing was held at the time. Few "serious writers" wrote for children; it was a field reserved mostly for financially needy women and hacks of both sexes. Only adult works achieved real literary recognition. Her adult works may have interested her more, but they are not as exceptional as her works for children; though they maintain the reader's interest, they are not outstanding as her best children's works are. Above all, the adult works are interesting for the contrast they establish between the "children's friend" and the lesser-known A. M. Barnard or L. M. Alcott or the anonymous writer for adults.

In this rather smaller number of works Alcott still shows a range of accomplishments. *Moods* was her first and favorite novel for adults, a sentimental novel dealing at least in part with divorce, an almost unthinkable social disposition at the time; *Hospital Sketches* is a collection of episodes taken from her Civil War experiences, which show her journalist's eye for detail and her ear for the speech patterns of plain, simple folk; *Work* is her domestic novel about the problems of working women in her time; and finally, *A Modern Mephistophiles* is a novel that is both sentimental and gothic. The most startling of these works is the collection of gothic thrillers—some short stories, some novellas—that was discovered by Leona Rostenberg and Madeleine Stern during World War II, but only collected and reissued in 1975 and 1976. All of Alcott's adult works show a more complex view of life than her children's books allow; the lives portrayed in these works are frequently sordid, dull, or otherwise unsatisfying, and the families cruel, cold, and broken. Her children's books were optimistic and inviting not because Alcott did not know or was not capable of writing of the more unpleasant, even revolting aspects of human existence; it was only in her works for adults, presumably, that her public, sometimes not knowing that it was the "children's friend" who was producing them, could accept this more comprehensive view of life.

Hospital Sketches

Hospital Sketches (1863) was for Alcott the first widespread public recognition of her skill as a writer. She was thirty years old when she served as an army nurse in Washington, D.C. She had long been a writer, especially of sentimental stories which kept her family sheltered, fed, and warm but which attracted little public attention. These stories appeared anonymously or pseudonymously in weekly newspapers which were never meant to be showcases of high, serious literature of any lasting importance. Alcott's career as a writer was not progressing as she wished it would. There were few other roles for women at the time; as she describes her choices at the beginning of *Hospital Sketches,* they were writing; teaching, which she had also tried; marriage, which seemed unlikely at her age; acting, which was out of the question for a well-bred woman; or nursing. As the Civil War opened, the call to action on behalf of a worthy reform movement, the abolition of slavery, offered her only endless bandage-rolling and sock-knitting for the "boys" in military service. As an heretofore active supporter of abolitionism, Alcott was hardly satisfied by such passive activities on behalf of the cause. When Dorothea Dix issued her call for women to serve as nurses in Union Army hospitals, Alcott volunteered.

Hospital Sketches is a thinly fictionalized collection of episodes about her short, but intense six weeks as an army nurse. In it, she relates her decision to volunteer, her journey from Boston to Washington by train and ferry, her work as a nurse, and her impressions of the doctors, nurses, chaplains, and soldiers that she met, as well as some description of Washington life and manners. Alcott served at the Union Hotel Hospital at a significant time during the Civil War. Shortly after she arrived, the Union forces were badly defeated at the battle of Fredericksburg, which resulted in a large number of wounded for whom Washington, D.C., was the closest source of medical attention. Some of the casualties waited two or three days for their wounds to be tended, either in the mud of the battlefield or sitting in the halls of the hospital. Alcott's first experience with battle injuries was therefore particularly intense, both because of the large number of patients and their dire conditions. She was also in Washington when the Emancipation Proclamation went into effect, on New Year's Day, 1863. She had the opportunity to observe southern blacks in Washington, and to compare their character, to their detriment, with northern blacks she had known in New England.

The experience was a nerveracking one for Alcott, an effect which comes through in the narrative. Alcott chose the name "Tribulation Periwinkle" for her fictional persona, a name which aptly captures the ambivalence of her nursing experience. On the one hand, the surname Periwinkle is light-hearted, humorous, almost a Dickensian name; indeed, the humor comes through in her jokes about the "P" family; all the "youthful P.s filled the pod of futurity with achievements whose brilliancy eclipsed the glories of the present and the past."[1] On the other hand, Tribulation suggests the difficulty of life in general, and of this nursing experience in particular. Alcott had never been far away from home by herself, and the journey would have been trying even under the best of circumstances; but it was wartime, conveyances were crowded, and a woman unattended could be an easy victim for pickpockets and ruffians. And the hospital where Alcott was stationed was hardly the kind that Dorothea Dix or Florence Nightingale would have approved. It was, as its name implied, a hotel converted into a hospital, without the equipment, the facilities, or the sanitation to heal; in fact, a stay in such a hospital might exacerbate illness or injury rather than cure it. Finally, a well-bred Victorian woman, Alcott had nonetheless to tend to the physical needs of the soldiers, washing wounds, changing dressings and clothing, and attending surgical procedures. Her reaction as she records it in *Hospital Sketches* is literally unspeakable: ". . . to scrub some dozen lords of creation at a moment's notice, was really—really—" (35). Though she "corked up her feelings, and returned to the path of duty" (34), and "scrubbed away like any tidy parent on a Saturday night" (36), her sense of delicacy must have been severely offended.

This dual emphasis, both on the humor of the situation and on its more tragic, horrific qualities, is clear in the characterization of two of her favorite soldiers, the Little Sergeant and John the blacksmith, both of whom she describes at length. The Sergeant would at first seem to be a rather pitiful figure, having lost an arm and a leg, but his sense of humor at his plight and his willingness to play the clown in his ward are the source of much of the book's humor. For example, when Nurse Periwinkle seeks to comfort him on the amputation of his arm, he jokes, "Lord! What a scramble there'll be for arms and legs, when we old boys come out of our graves, on the Judgement Day: wonder if we shall get our own again? If we do, my leg will have to tramp from Fredericksburg, my arm from here, I suppose, and meet my body, wherever it may be" (37).

In contrast to the Sergeant is John the blacksmith, "the manliest man" (59) in Nurse Periwinkle's care, who has returned from his first and last battle with a fatal stomach wound. He is beyond medical care and is in the hospital to die. The interest that Alcott invests in John's character makes him sound like a romantic hero: "bashful as brave, yet full of excellencies and fine aspirations, which, having no power to express themselves in words, seemed to have bloomed into his character and made him what he was" (59). In fact, he is the model for David Sterling, the lover of her later novel *Work,* who also dies in the Civil War. John is the sole support of his widowed mother and younger brother and sister, and he enlisted not for vainglory, but because he "wanted the right thing done" (60). His death is a painful and slow one, and Nurse Periwinkle acts the part of "the poor substitute for mother, wife, or sister" (58), holding his hand as he struggles to breathe. He dies as the sun rises on the next day, his hand firmly grasping his nurse's; subsequently his body suggests the nobility of his life: "a most heroic figure, lying there stately and still as the statue of some young knight asleep upon his tomb" (64). John is the real focus of attention in the book; he is the uncomplaining, otherwise unsung hero about whom readers in the North were desperate to read. Though they would have been interested in almost any information about their "boys," that Alcott had made a coherent story out of an otherwise rambling account of miscellaneous events made the book all the more interesting.

As her friend Julia Ward Howe did in the "Battle Hymn of the Republic," Louisa May Alcott made the Civil War into a struggle between God and the forces of evil over the issue of slavery. Though the devils in the South are not in evidence in the book, the "soldiers of the Lord" (57) are, and it was at least partly this analogy of John the blacksmith, the Little Sergeant, and others, fighting a holy war that made the book a popular success in the North. Nurse Periwinkle herself responds to the call to war as to Gabriel's trumpet, and sees her work as part of the great mission to help the North win. The job of nursing is an important one, and as she leaves for her job, her head is full of "all manner of high thoughts and heroic purposes 'to do or die,'—perhaps both" (13). Though Alcott plainly asserts "that these Sketches are not romance" (21), she does infuse these stories with enough of the trappings of high heroism that the book takes on a chivalric, almost apocalyptic quality. At the end of the book reference to Sir Thomas More's adjuration to his family as he was facing execution to "be merrie in God" (101) is particularly apt. Though there were humorous, "merrie" aspects of Alcott's nursing experience and though one could be assured of God's continued support for the just and the right, God's soldier might be facing death, a frightful prospect, even if also a martyrdom by which he might achieve sainthood.

Compared to that other popular work about the struggle over slavery, *Uncle Tom's Cabin* (1852), *Hospital Sketches* shows Alcott's skill in controlling language without the excesses of sentimental effusion that characterize Stowe's book. In fact, the last chapter of *Hospital Sketches* is devoted to a description of the functioning of an army hospital "for the benefit of any ardent damsel whose patriotic fancy may have surrounded hospital life with a halo of charms" (67). The food is bad, the hours long, the Union Hotel Hospital unhealthful, the chaplains hardly comforting, some of the doctors indifferent to pain, the grieving relatives of the wounded an actual hindrance to their comfort and recovery. This frankness and emphasis on stark reality in a journalistic manner contrast sharply with the more heroic, more novelistic portions of the book, yet both contributed to its popularity and literary noteworthiness.

Moods

Of all the books she ever wrote, both for adults and children, *Moods* was Alcott's favorite. She wrote it as Jo March did her first novel, falling into a "vortex" of fevered composition which consumed all her energy and attention for days on end. She began work on the novel in 1860, revised and submitted it for publication in 1864. When, after trying other publishers, Alcott submitted the manuscript to A. K. Loring, he advised her to cut its length in half so that it might be printed in one volume. She ruthlessly sacrificed ten chapters and much of the description of landscape and character. The result left both her and her critics dissatisfied.

In 1881, after she had become rich and famous as a writer for children, Loring returned the copyright to her. Her current publisher, Thomas Niles of Roberts Brothers, was willing to publish a new edition, with many of the eliminated chapters restored and the others revised. As Alcott says in the preface to this edition, "Several chapters have been omitted, several of the original ones restored; and those that remain have been pruned of as much fine writing as could be done without destroying the youthful spirit of the little romance."[2]

Though the difference between the two editions is considerable, the story is basically the same. Eighteen-year-old Sylvia Yule is the heroine, a young woman whose life is ruled by the moods of the title. As the motto from Emerson on the 1864 title page suggests, such a life so dominated is not entirely satisfactory because of its narrowness and instability: "Life is a train of moods like a string of beads; and as we pass through them they prove to be many colored lenses, which paint the world their own hue, and each shows us only what lies in its own focus." Accordingly, Sylvia's life is out of focus; she follows her feelings rather than her intellect or moral principles, a course of action Alcott clearly finds misguided. She is alternately depressed and ebullient, languid and energetic. The alteration makes her uncontrollable and yet attractive.

As Sylvia is just entering upon womanhood, she is offered a choice between two men, one whom she loves, the other who loves her. The first, Adam Warwick, is another of the love interests in Alcott's books who is modeled after Thoreau. He is described as "broad-shouldered, strong-limbed, and bronzed by wind and weather. A massive head, covered with waves of ruddy brown hair, gray eyes that seemed to pierce through all disguises, an eminent nose, and a beard. . . . Power, intellect, and courage were stamped on face and figure, making him the manliest man Sylvia had ever seen" (50). Sylvia's brother describes him as "violently virtuous . . . masterful . . . bent on living out his aspirations and beliefs at any cost . . . [he] leads a life of sternest integrity" (51). As Sylvia later discovers, he is particularly destructive of the people he loves: "He clings to principles; persons are but animated facts or ideas; he seizes, searches, uses them, and when they have no more for him, drops them like the husk, whose kernel he has secured; passing on to find and study other samples without regret, but with unabated zeal" (248). Sylvia falls in love with him almost at once. Though he is strong-minded and she is not, they both share an immoderation in their ways of life that attracts them to each other. Adam decides to leave with the mutual love unacknowledged and unrequited.

His absence leaves the field of love clear for his best friend, Geoffrey Moor, a near neighbor of Sylvia's. She finds in him what she hopes is true friendship, but he mistakes her affection for and frankness with him for reciprocated love. In character, Moor is the direct opposite of Warwick, "much slighter, and . . . in every gesture the unconscious grace and ease of the gentlemen born. A most attractive face, with its broad brow, serene eyes, and a cordial smile about the mouth. A sweet, strong nature. . . . Inward tranquility seemed his" (50). Sylvia finds him kinder, more mature, more sedate than Warwick was with her. At first she turns down his suit, but when it becomes clear that Warwick will not come back, she rationalizes that what she feels for Moor is "safe," mistakes deepening friendship for love, and consents to marry him, hoping that his love for her will teach her to be steady and less capricious.

Warwick confronts the two after their marriage and divines the increasing misery of their life together. Sylvia finally confesses to Moor her love for Warwick; he decides to leave her for a year to see if she can learn to love him truly. She does; but on Moor's voyage back to her, Warwick, who has accompanied him during his exile, is drowned. The couple is reunited, sadder for the loss of their friend, but wiser and surer of the mutuality of their love.

At this point, the novel nearly finished, Alcott's two versions offer radically different endings for Sylvia. In the 1864 edition she dies of tuberculosis, cultivated by the long suffering and wasting away during her marriage and after her separation from Moor. She concludes that her life has not been a loss, for she has taught Warwick gentleness in loving him, has given Moor the inspiration to write great poetry out of his grief, and has atoned for her moodiness toward her family by caring for them as a sister would, scattering affection and sunshine about the house. Moor returns home to nurse her through her last few months, and she dies in his arms, going to heaven to meet Warwick who has gone before her.

The romance and sentimentality of this ending is further underscored by the reason for Warwick's inability to marry Sylvia when they first fall in love. In an opening chapter is a description of his previous engagement to a hot-blooded, unprincipled Cuban beauty who has seduced him into a promise of marriage. In his attempts to extricate himself from this unworthy alliance, he promises to wait a year to see if the lady can learn integrity. The year is not up when he meets Sylvia; he tells no one about the Cuban lady, but goes away until he can honorably answer her love. In another chapter, missing from the 1881 edition, Sylvia meets the woman and is led to believe that Warwick will undoubtedly marry this rival upon his return to her. Sylvia therefore rebounds to Moor. The exotic setting in Cuba, the stilted language with which Warwick and his lady converse— "Only a month betrothed, and yet so cold and gloomy, Adam!"—"Only a month betrothed and yet so fond and jealous, Otilla!" (8)—and Warwick's grim taciturnity about confessing the turmoil in which Otilla has left him make him such a colossus of mystery and temper that he is too large for life. It is no wonder that Sylvia considers her feelings for Moor "safe" as compared to the possibility of a life with Warwick. In the figure of Warwick, in the Cuban chapters, and in the 1864 ending the reader can see traces of the "thrillers," full of gothic romance and intrigue, that Alcott was composing at the time she first wrote and published *Moods*.

The 1881 edition, revised after Alcott had had much experience and success with writing domestic fiction, shows the influence of those more moderate kinds of composition. With the Cuban motif eliminated from its strategic place at the beginning of the novel, Warwick's character is cut down to size. Though he is still grand and masterful, he has a sense of humor which comes through more clearly in the revision, and his laconic presence comes not from his wish to keep a deep, dark secret, but rather from being socially ungraceful. Sylvia chooses to marry Moor from faulty information about Warwick's inaccessibility; Warwick confronts her with his love because he has not yet heard she is married. Finally, at the end of this version, Sylvia chooses to live; though she falls ill when first separated from her husband, she wills herself back to health and happiness and learns to accept her loving duty to Moor as his wife. Though the ending of the 1881 edition may still be sweet and sentimental, it is much less over-wrought with Sylvia happy and alive than with her angelical transfigura-tion in death. Alcott's revisions make the book much more readable and believable; the 1881 edition is domestic fiction rather than gothic thriller.

The focus in this later version is much more clearly on Sylvia. With the background chapters on Warwick's Cuban involvement eliminated, the focus remains on him only as he relates to her and her moods. Actually, Sylvia is not as preposterous a character as Alcott would have the reader believe. Alcott claims that her personality is the result of her parents' unhappy marriage and her inheritance of their diverse character traits: "From her father she received pride, intellect, and will; from her mother passion, imagination, and . . . fateful melancholy. . . . These conflicting temperaments, with all their aspirations, attributes, and inconsistencies, were woven into a nature fair and faulty; ambitious, yet not self-reliant; sensitive, yet not keen-sighted. These two masters ruled soul and body, warring against each other, making Sylvia an enigma to herself and her life a train of moods" (115–16). However, this description, but for the Victorian genetic theory Alcott applies to Sylvia's heritage, might just as easily fit Jo March or any other lively young woman of the period who found Victorian strictures on female activity intolerable. Sylvia is young;

much of what Alcott describes as Sylvia's caprice might just as easily be explained as the normal reactions to circumstances of an inexperienced teen-ager. Sylvia is only uncontrollably moody as compared to the rigid, confined model of womanhood to which she is bound to compare herself.

Alcott obviously focused more clearly on moods as the theme of the 1881 edition because of the critics' estimation of the 1864 edition that its real theme was marriage. In the revision, marriage, or more generally the relations between men and women, is still central, although it is not as primary as in the 1864 edition, especially with Warwick's nearly fatal misstep in Cuba eliminated. But Sylvia's problems do not arise until she confuses love and marriage. At the beginning of the book she longs for friendship, especially with a man. But, as she recognizes, when she brings up such an idea, "no sooner do I mention the word friendship than people nod wisely and look as if they said, 'Oh, yes, every one knows what that sort of thing amounts to'" (36). It is precisely because Moor cannot discern the difference between earnest friendship and erotic love that he proposes to Sylvia in the first place; for the same confused reason she accepts him later as lover and husband. It would seem that Alcott is lamenting that Victorian men and women were pressured into romantic relationships whether or not their love was suited for marriage.

Sylvia's, Moor's, and Warwick's mistakes are discussed in one of the most remarkable scenes in the book, where their situation is minutely dissected under the guise of gossip at an after-dinner party about another woman who has left her husband for another man. The assembled guests discuss whether the woman should have left her husband, should marry the lover, or should live alone. Sylvia defends the woman by saying, "She should have honestly decided which she loved, have frankly told the husband the mistake both had made, and demanded her liberty. If the lover was worthy, have openly married him and borne the world's censures. If not worthy, have stood alone, an honest woman in God's eyes, whatever the blind world might have thought" (200). Warwick's solution is slightly different and even more radical:

I would begin at the beginning, and teach young people that marriage is not the only aim and end of life, yet would fit them for a sacrament too high and holy to be profaned by a light word or thought. Show them how to be worthy of it and how to wait for it. Give them a law of life both cheerful and sustaining; a law that shall keep them hopeful if single, sure that here or hereafter they will find that other self and be accepted by it; happy if wedded, for their own integrity of heart will teach them to know the true god when he comes, and keep them loyal to the last. . . . Because two persons love, it is not always safe or wise for them to marry, nor need it necessarily wreck their peace to live apart. (200–201)

The voice of wisdom, as opposed to the social iconoclasm that both Sylvia and Warwick express, is represented by Moor's cousin, who suggests that if both husband and wife

find that they do not love, the sooner they part the wiser; if one alone makes the discovery the case is sadder still, and harder for either to decide . . . . the wife, having promised to guard another's happiness, should sincerely endeavor to do so, remembering that in making the joy of others we often find our own, and that having made so great a mistake the others should not bear all the loss . . . . she should leave no effort unmade, no self-denial unexacted, till she has proved beyond all doubt that it is impossible to be a true wife. Then, and not till then, has she the right to dissolve the tie that has become a sin, because where no love lives inevitable suffering and sorrow enter in, falling not only upon guilty parents, but the innocent children who may be given them . . . . I would have the lover suffer and wait; sure that, however it may fare with him, he will be the richer and the better for having known the joy and pain of love. (201–203)

Moor takes no particular stand on the matter. Though Sylvia's sister puts him in the hypothetical position of the husband, he simply and earnestly responds, "I love but few, and those few are my world; so do not try me too hardly, Sylvia," to which she equivocally responds, "I shall do my best, Geoffrey" (204).

Though Sylvia follows the cousin's advice in the end and learns "to live by principle, not impulse, and this made it both sweet and possible for love and duty to go hand in hand" (359), she does not do so without incurring the gossip of the world by first separating from Moor. She becomes, as Alcott categorizes her, like Hester Prynne: "She had joined that sad sisterhood called disappointed women. . . . Unhappy wives; mistaken or forsaken lovers; meek souls, who make life a long penance for the sins of others; gifted creatures kindled into fitful brilliance . . ." (260). Though Sylvia chooses this difficult course, she does not do so automatically, without hearing and seriously considering the other courses open to her, no matter how socially unacceptable they might be. Alcott defies the constraints of fictional propriety at the time, especially those of popular women's fiction, and faces the difficult issue of unhappy marriages with unusual frankness. She offers no simple-minded solutions to its difficulty.

Perhaps the issue was important to her because of the unhappiness of her parents' marriage and her mother's continuing devotion to her father despite their problems. Martha Saxton suggests that, since Alcott began writing the novel shortly after her sister's marriage when she herself apparently had some unsuitable beaux, the story was inspired by the difference she perceived between her sister's husband John Pratt and Alcott's own love, Henry David Thoreau.[3] Certainly the relationships between men and women, including both love and friendship, were always a concern for her (as with Jo March and Teddy Laurence) and inspired her interest in women's rights and suffrage as she observed the inequality of the sexes. In any case, marriage is as much a theme as moodiness in the 1864 edition, and remains so in the revision of 1881.

All in all, the novel is an uneven one, especially in the 1864 edition where the ragged edges are still visible from the sections which Alcott wrenched out. The sections of the book set in Cuba are too exotic for the more realistic parts of the novel, and Alcott did well to eliminate them in the 1881 revision. The later work is much more even in characterization and plotting, but Alcott sacrifices none of the effectiveness of the discussion about marriage and divorce in her reworking.

Gothic "Potboilers"

Jo March's first literary efforts were so unlike Louisa Alcott's known works that readers and critics naturally assumed that Alcott was fictionalizing her autobiographical heroine here. As with Jo, Alcott had a history of writing sensational plays for herself and her sisters to perform. The play that the March girls present on Christmas night for their friends, *The Witch's Curse, an Operatic Tragedy,* is much like the plays that Alcott wrote for her sisters when they were young, as *Comic Tragedies* (Boston: Roberts Brothers, 1893), a collection of those early plays, verifies. So Alcott had experience in composing in the lurid, gothic style. It therefore makes sense when Jo March writes the "romantic, and somewhat pathetic" "Rival Painters" for the *Spread Eagle* (*Little Women,* pp. 165–66), though such works might be thought out of character for Alcott herself. Jo finds herself even more involved in this kind of writing when she goes to New York in the second half of the book and finds that writing stories for *The Blarneystone Banner* and *The Weekly Volcano* is quite lucrative. She had vowed to go to New York not only to break ties with Laurie but also to gather material for her writing, which she does with a vengeance. When an editor advises her to write stories which are "short and spicy, never mind the moral," she obeys, finding incidents to write about in newspapers and history, and in researching such horrific subjects as poisoning. The writing excites her, the money is gratifying, and there is always a ready market for the stories.

Of course, the terribly moral Professor Bhaer objects to such "sensation stories," claiming that writers "haf no right to put poison in the sugarplum, and let the small ones eat it" (*Little Women*, 379). Though she permits Jo to carry on in this lurid style for some time, Alcott reminds us at the beginning that such writing harms the author, especially the female author, as well as the reader, for it destroys the delicate sensibilities that are a woman's special purview. When Professor Bhaer burns one of the scandal sheets, Jo decides to follow his example and burns all her writing from the past three months.

Like Jo, Alcott published her thrillers without a name or under a pseudonym, A. M. Barnard. As a consequence, these stories remained unidentified until Leona Rostenberg, a rare book collector, found a series of letters between Alcott and James R. Elliott, publisher of *The Flag of Our Union*. The letters revealed the names of three of the stories and Alcott's pseudonym. Further investigation revealed several other stories written for Elliott and for *Frank Leslie's Illustrated Newspaper*, which Rostenberg reported on in 1943.[4] In 1975 and 1976 Madeleine Stern edited two collections of these stories, hitherto hidden in some obscure journals of Civil War vintage.

Like Jo, Alcott wrote the stories for the money and kept their author anonymous in order to protect her reputation as a more serious, more strictly literary writer. In 1854 *The Saturday Evening Gazette* published Alcott's first short story, "The Rival Prima Donnas" under the pseudonym of Flora Fairfield. Like the later thrillers, this is a tale of gory revenge, this time of one actress against another. Alcott later dramatized the story and tried to get it produced by a Boston theater company.

She first submitted a thriller to *Frank Leslie's Illustrated Newspaper* in 1862 to compete for a hundred dollar prize, which she subsequently won. Frank Leslie and James R. Elliott of *The Flag of Our Union* both solicited manuscripts from her, which she insisted be published either anonymously or under a pseudonym, A. M. Barnard. The origin of the pseudonym is not known, although Stern, in the preface to her first collection of reprinted thrillers, suggests that A. M. stood for Abigail May, Alcott's mother's maiden name, and that Barnard was borrowed from Henry Barnard, a friend of the family and a well-known educator from Connecticut.[5] Only one of the thrillers, "A Whisper in the Dark," in *Frank Leslie's Illustrated Newspaper*, appeared with Alcott's own name on it. Stern speculates that Alcott permitted her name to be used because in the story the heroine is a victim and does no evil herself.

The stories mainly concern women who have found life difficult, in any number of ways. Virginie Varens of "V. V.: or, Plots and Counterplots" is an orphan with a jealous guardian who murders her husband on her wedding night and forces her to conceal the truth. She is also a dancer, hardly a respectable profession for a Victorian woman. Jean Muir of "Behind a Mask" is thirty years old and single, born out of wedlock, too old to be an actress, but still with enough talent to appear much younger in order to woo an older man with a title and a fortune. Cecelia Stein of "A Marble Woman: or, The Mysterious Model" is also an orphan, forced to live with an unaffectionate, reclusive sculptor for a guardian, who punishes her in return for the love her mother left unrequited in him. All the women are victorious, even Virginie Varens, who outwits those who wish to punish her by committing suicide, the ultimate triumph. The women have nerves of steel and are cool even in the closest call. They triumph over, rather than succumb to, the roles prescribed for women in the Victorian period.

Alcott frequently sets her scene in Europe, or in an unidentified but elegant American location, as in "The Marble Woman." The scene is set in gothic magnificence, full of colorful, ornate furnishings and beautiful, exotic people of the gothic mode, aristocrats and aesthetes, especially of the young, handsome, rich, unmarried male variety. The stories touch on the themes of insanity, imprisonment, and especially disguise. In "Perilous Play" Alcott has her characters take hashish; this is only one of three recorded instances of hashish mentioned in nineteenth-century American fiction; one other occurs in Alcott's *A Modern Mephistophiles,* which Elliott declined to publish in its original form in 1866, saying it was too sensational, but which Roberts Brothers published in 1877 in the No Name series, after Alcott had rewritten it and toned it down.

These are not the moral stories for the young that the reader expects from the author of children's novels. No good little women are found, at least none of any interest and certainly none as main characters. The simple, everyday style of the children's novels is also absent here, for Alcott's penchant for elegant detail and overwrought dialogue and incident is given full play. Her experience in the theater, both attending plays and reworking short stories into drama, served her well here, for she vividly defines character and manipulates complicated plots of disguise and diabolical revenge with consistency, ease, and vigor.

Alcott kept up her production of thrillers until the publication of *Little Women.* By this time she had found the formula for financial and critical success in her writing. She no longer needed to produce the thrillers for money, though when given the chance to revert to the gothic style, she did with *A Modern Mephistophiles*. She also kept her skill at subversive plotting in the small incidents of her children's novels, especially in the March family novels, which subtly undercut the seemingly loving and harmonious surface. Alcott also had a reputation as a morally acceptable writer for children to protect, which her thrillers threatened. And she was busy and frequently unwell after the publication of *Little Women*, so that she had little time to indulge in the gothic for the fun of it.

Work

Work: A Story of Experience is Alcott's most successful adult novel. She started writing it in 1860, at the same time she was working on *Moods*, but unlike the earlier novel, she did not publish it early in her career. In 1873 when Henry Ward Beecher asked Alcott for an adult novel to be serialized in his monthly magazine, *The Christian Register*, she went back to the manuscript and revised it, although not as drastically as she had revised *Moods*. Perhaps because she was not as attached to it as she had been to the earlier novel, *Work* is a much more successful book. It does not indulge at such great length in fine writing and metaphysical considerations, as does *Moods*, and its characters are much more realistic, much more in proportion to normal human nature than the overwrought Sylvia and gigantic Warwick in the earlier novel.

It is the story of twenty-one-year-old orphan, Christie Devon, who decides with admirable fortitude and energy to make her own living in the world instead of marrying or remaining dependent on her aunt and uncle. She leaves her family with high hopes and finds work first as a domestic, then as an actress, a governess, a companion to an invalid girl, and a seamstress. She goes through these early jobs quite rapidly, each one in the space of a chapter; in fact, the early part of the novel is episodic in form. It is not until Christie has settled down as a seamstress and has met her friend Rachel that the novel becomes the domestic type of fiction that a reader might expect of Alcott. Christie befriends Rachel, a poor, timid woman whom she meets while both work at a dressmaker's shop. When the rumor is confirmed that Rachel is a "fallen" woman (the circumstances of the fall are not revealed), she is fired, and Christie loses her job also for remaining friendly toward Rachel. Rachel is gratified by Christie's moral support and, vowing eternal friendship, sets out on her own, in spite of Christie's entreaties to stay with her. Christie continues to work at whatever sewing jobs she can find; she slowly becomes poorer, hungrier, lonelier, and more and more depressed, until she contemplates suicide. Fortuitously, Rachel appears at the very moment Christie is about to throw herself into the river, and rescues her. She sends Christie to the home of a friend, a comical washerwoman named Mrs. Wilkins, who takes on the care of such destitute women as Christie whenever the need arises. Mrs. Wilkins introduces Christie to the Reverend Thomas Power, a charismatic preacher who also is very much involved with charity cases like Christie. He arranges for Christie to live with a widow and her son, as a companion to the woman.

Here is the real interest of the story, for the son is the love interest in the book, yet another version of Henry David Thoreau. David Sterling is a florist, a man saddened by a woman in his past. Though Christie romanticizes about him before she meets him and assumes that the woman was a lover who jilted him, she finds, not the sentimentally gloomy man she expects, but rather, "Only a broad-shouldered, brown-bearded man, with an old hat and coat, trousers tucked into his boots, fresh mould on the hand he had given her to shake, and the cheeriest voice she had ever heard."[6] As Christie and David become more and more attracted to each other, Christie tries to make David into a hero, but he is distinctly unheroic: "he *won't* be ambitious. I try to stir him up, for he has talents; I've found that out: but he won't seem to care for any thing but watching over his mother, reading his old books, and making flowers bloom double when they ought to be single" (253). Though their attraction is challenged by other suitable partners for each of them, they finally declare their love. The Civil War intervenes, and the two are married just before David goes off to battle and Christie to nurse in an army hospital. David dies in battle, leaving Christie pregnant.

In the final scene Christie is shown living with her baby daughter, mother-in-law, and sister-in-law who is the wronged Rachel, the sister whom David unfairly exiled from his family for her elopement with an unworthy lover. Fortunately, David reconciled with her before he went off to the war, for she was the woman whose memory so blighted his life. Christie manages the florist business and has turned her hand to social work, helping women to be independent wage earners, no matter what their social status.

The novel is an autobiographical one in many ways. Though Alcott was no orphan, she did find it difficult to make her way as an independent working woman, and she did try all the occupations that Christie does, with the exceptions of wife and florist. She tried domestic service; the black servant with whom Christie worked is modeled after Harriet Tubman, whom Alcott knew. Alcott was also a sort of governess, a teacher at various periods in her life. She tried the theater as Christie did—in fact, the name Christie Devon appears as a member of the stock company of the Boston Theatre Company in the 1855–56 season;[7] it may have been Alcott's stage name. She was a Civil War nurse and a companion to a sick young girl on her first trip to Europe; she also knew Theodore Parker, after whom the fictional Thomas Power, the preacher in *Work,* is modeled. She was romantically interested in Henry David Thoreau, the model for David Sterling, complete with Thoreau's difficulty with women, his love of flowers and learning, and his flute.

The dominant emotions of this quasi-autobiography are loneliness and frustration. That life was difficult for Alcott is clearly evident, as when Christie (her counterpart in the novel) becomes ill with no one to look after her. There are four suicides and suicide attempts in the book: Matty Stone, mentioned at the beginning of the book, who had tried "to crush and curb her needs and aspirations till the struggle grew too hard, and then in a fit of despair [to] end her life, and leave a tragic story to haunt their quiet river" (12); Helen Carroll, the young girl whom Christie nurses, who dies because of the hereditary madness which she knows will eventually make life unlivable for her; and both Rachel and Christie, who contemplate suicide when caring for themselves, both physically and emotionally, becomes too difficult and they are both so poor and ill that depression is inevitable. Fortunately, both are saved by a benevolent bystander; in Christie's case it is Rachel.

The frustration with life for such women as Christie and Alcott herself is clear. Though they are willing to work hard and take care of themselves, the nineteenth-century world will not let them; no one cares if they become ill or destitute or simply lonely. The case for women like Rachel, who make a mistake with one man but are determined to reform, is much more dire. They are universally shunned, with no possibility of ever becoming respectable women again. When Rachel is thrown out of work, she lashes out at her former employer: "It's no use for such as me . . . . better go back to the old life, for there are kinder hearts among the sinners than among the saints, and no one can live without a bit of love. Your Magdelen Asylums are penitentiaries, not homes; I won't go to any of them. Your piety isn't worth much, for though you read in your Bible how the Lord treated a poor soul like me, yet when I stretch out my hand to you for help, not one of all you virtuous, Christian women dare take it and keep me from a life that's worse than hell" (139).

Alcott was certainly not a woman in Rachel's situation; but her sympathy for such women, especially for those who must support themselves, is obvious. Her own isolation when she was just beginning to work was parallel to the dilemma that both Rachel and Christie face, in their willingness to work and yet in the dearth of socially acceptable situations they could find. Alcott shows a kind of paranoia in Rachel's and Christie's problems, in that she sees that life for women is always a battle. But she also articulates a certain optimism and acceptance of trouble, for both Rachel and Christie have happy lives in the end. Rachel is reunited with her brother and mother, and she has as a sister-in-law a woman whom she has loved even before their familial connection. Christie does have a marriage, albeit a brief one, a child, and a happy home. And as Mrs. Wilkins says, " 'Pears to me trouble is a kind of mellerin' process, and ef you take it kindly it doos you good, and you learn to be glad of it" (195). If trouble is inevitable, at least Alcott and her heroines learn to accept it gracefully.

Through all the trouble that Christie experiences, her one salvation is work. In fact, throughout her life and books, Alcott consistently recommends hard, honest work as virtuous and redemptive and even compensatory for the lack of love and happiness. Christie rescues herself from her suicidal depression by finding ways to be helpful around the Wilkins household and by agreeing to go to the Sterlings. She recovers from the shock of David's death by devoting herself to her child and by becoming a philanthropist of sorts, helping other women. She finds that some work is not as wholesome as others; the theater, while it pleases her, also degrades those finer sensitivities that the Victorians thought belonged especially to women. But no work, not even domestic service, is beneath dignity; as Christie says, "I'll put my pride in my pocket, and go out to service. Housework I like, and can do well, thanks to Aunt Betsey. I never thought it degradation to do it for her, so why should I mind doing it for others if they pay for it?" (16).

But it is the amount of pay that is the rub. Alcott, though she may be somewhat simplistic about the psychological value of work, recognizes that women's labor, no matter how noble or vital it may be in the social order, is not paid well enough; at least part of the dignity of work comes from sufficient money earned in order to live decently. Christie's plight as a free-lance seamstress is particularly distressing, since the women she works for are always trying to cheat her out of the money she has just earned. Alcott's sympathy for women in such predicaments is part of the reason why Christie's philanthropy at the end of the novel is devoted to the causes of working women.

Though Christie's life illustrates the value of work, it also illustrates, as no other Alcott novel does, the realistic relationships between men and women. In the course of the novel Christie has three different suitors: Joe

Butterfield, a farmer whom Christie rejects because life with him would make her into a "farmer's household drudge" (12), and because she expects more from life than the limited possibilities that life as her aunt and uncle see it would offer her; Philip Fletcher, a rich invalid who proposes to Christie because he thinks she would amuse him and because, with his money, he thinks that such a marriage would be doing her a favor—marriage to him without the love she so desperately craves would be marrying for a living, as Mrs. Wilkins says; and finally David Sterling, whose courtship with Christie is hampered by her attempts to make him a hero, a man more than life-sized.

But the Henry David Thoreau substitute that Alcott creates here is just a man, although an unusual one in his love of flowers, his care of his mother, and his attempts to atone for his unjust treatment of his sister by helping other women such as Christie. He is no wild romantic like Adam Warwick in *Moods,* no berserker bad boy like Dan Kean in *Little Men* and *Jo's Boys.* Both Christie's and David's problems are openly presented and dealt with as human beings would deal with such difficulties. Though Christie and David are not married long, as least Alcott could bring herself to imagine her heroine-surrogate taking the fateful step into matrimony, especially since the more sexual aspects of the relationship between Christie and David are kept discreetly offstage.

But by killing David off in a summary though noble way, Alcott has placed Christie in the usual safety of a circle of women, as in the artist colony in *An Old-Fashioned Girl* and in the cozy circle of mother and sisters in *Little Women.* Although Alcott recognizes that there is strength to be gained in women's solidarity, she does not also recognize that there is long-term strength in relationships with men. Marriage is dependence, conjugal relationships unsatisfactory.

A Modern Mephistophiles

Alcott wrote the original version of *A Modern Mephistophiles* in 1866, at the same time that she was writing the best of her thrillers. James R. Elliott of *The Flag of Our Union* had asked her for a long story, of twenty-four chapters; when she finally submitted it, he found it too thrilling to publish even in his sensational newspaper. Alcott laid the manuscript aside and reconsidered it in late 1876, when Thomas Niles of Roberts Brothers asked her for a contribution to their No Name series of books by popular authors which were published anonymously. The manuscript came to mind for two reasons: first, Alcott would be able to write in the gothic mode about sensational evil and yet protect her reputation as a children's writer of unexceptionable virtues, since her authorship would remain a secret; second, the year before she had read Goethe's *Faust* with which she had been mightily impressed.

The story concerns a young man, Felix Canaris, who aspires to be a poet, a well-known and successful one at that. At the point where the story begins he has received a rejection from a publisher for his collection of poetry. He is destitute, alone, and on the point of suicide, when he is mysteriously befriended by an older, wealthy man, the Mephistophiles of the story, Jasper Helwyze. Helwyze makes an unexplained bargain with Canaris to help him in his career and see that he is successful as well as comfortably provided for as long as Canaris stays with him. After a year, Canaris is a published, acclaimed poet, the pet of fashionable society, and yet dissatisfied. He falls in love with an older woman, Helwyze's former beloved Olivia, who jilted Helwyze and has suffered just retribution in an ill-fated marriage, but now is a glamorous, wealthy widow. But Gladys, a young orphan whom Olivia has taken on as a protégé, has fallen in love with the attractive young poet, and Helwyze forces him to marry her.

The young couple move into Helwyze's country estate, the sour old man amusing himself by tormenting them. Gladys realizes that Helwyze's power over her husband is unwholesome, and she convinces Felix that they can make it on their own without the older man's support. Helwyze senses that he is losing control over the couple, and before they have a chance to leave, he invites Olivia, under the guise of renewed love for her, to stay with them at his home. Canaris is no longer tempted; he has fallen truly in love with Gladys. But so has Helwyze; he gives her hashish to help her sleep one night, and it affects her by bringing out a provocatively sexual side of her to which she gives full play in a series of theatrical tableaux during the evening's entertainment. Before she comes out of the spell Helwyze further probes her feelings about him using a kind of hypnosis. She reveals that she fears his love; in a more lucid moment later, Helwyze pleads for her love, but she promises only to pray for him. She is pregnant by her husband, and the couple look forward to starting out on their own; but Helwyze forces Canaris to reveal to his wife the secret that has kept the two men bound to each other: almost all of Canaris's published poetry is really Helwyze's. Canaris has almost no literary talent of his own.

Gladys does not lose her love for her husband, but she does go into labor prematurely; both she and her baby son die, promising to meet Canaris in heaven and admonishing both Canaris and Helwyze to forgive each other. Canaris is released from his bond to Helwyze and leaves him to lead a worthy life so that he can be prepared to meet Gladys in heaven; Helwyze suffers a paralytic stroke which will eventually result in his death, but only Olivia is left to take care of the remaining shell of a man.

The parallels to Goethe's *Faust* are numerous, especially to that part of the drama concerning Gretchen. Though Faust is an older man, more worldly-wise and experienced than Canaris, for the Gretchen episode he is rejuvenated into an attractive young man in order to seduce the young virtuous girl. Mephisto and Helwyze both use jewels to seduce the young women on behalf of Canaris and Faust, and like Goethe's Mephisto, Helwyze offers his victim worldly comforts and acclaim in return for his soul, in this case Canaris's art. Both Gretchen and Gladys are the source of divine salvation for their men, thereby aiding them to slip the bonds of their evil captors. Alcott pays homage to this debt to Goethe in the epigraph, "The Indescribable, / Here it is done: / The Woman-Soul leadeth us / Upward and on!"[8] The Woman-Soul, or in more modern translations the Eternal Feminine, in the person of Gladys saves Canaris by her love and her constant faith in God, as Gretchen saves Faust at the end of Goethe's work.

As in Goethe's poem, the devil tempts the man to inaction, rather than to action on his own behalf; in paralysis the man will be given all manner of worldly success, and his attempts at action will only fail. Felix Canaris is a poet, a man of words; when Goethe's Faust considers the Bible, he translates John 1:1 as "In the beginning was the act," rather than "In the beginning was the Word." For Felix, in the beginning are both word, his poetry, and act, his own authorship of it. His Mephistophiles, Helwyze, subverts both word and act by almost effortlessly convincing Canaris to publish Helwyze's poetry under his own name, thereby leaving him with no word of his own and a deceitful act. Thereafter, Canaris finds that he can no longer act on his own because of the secret Helwyze holds over him, nor can he produce words; all his attempts at composition produce only frustration. Only Gladys can inspire him to act on his own, both for his sake and for hers. This parallel concerning action and inaction with Goethe's work gives the book most of its intrigue and energy.

The character of Olivia is a difficult one to fit into the pattern that Goethe's *Faust* suggests in the novel; at one point, as Canaris and Gladys are wooing, Helwyze joins Olivia on a balcony overlooking them, describing them as "Mephistophiles and Martha looking on" (36). Though she is a sort of guardian to Gladys, Olivia fits the role of Helen much better than that of Martha, Gretchen's mother. She tempts Canaris as Faust is tempted by Helen, and is a pale imitation of the Woman-Soul realized more perfectly in Gladys, but a meaningful imitation nonetheless. Toward the end of the novel Gladys calls Olivia's attention to her power over Canaris; realizing that Gladys is right about the sinister reason for Helwyze's invitation to his home, Olivia agrees to stop tempting Canaris and promises to help Gladys escape with Canaris from Helwyze's clutches. And it is Olivia who is left behind to care for Helwyze in his debility, a faithful lover after all.

These are the most basic parallels to Goethe's masterpiece. There are many others, most of which are heavy-handed in Alcott's adaptation of them though effective sometimes in creating the mood of intrigue and malevolence in the book's atmosphere. For instance, Olivia says that Helwyze's perverse attitude toward life is a result of "a terrible fall" (26) which has injured him permanently and left him in incredible pain; Alcott here recalls the fall of Mephistophiles from heaven and his eternal damnation, but the device is an obvious one with no subtlety. The names Helwyze and Felix are obviously chosen for their suggestive value, though the other names of the characters are less so. At one point, Gladys is called "Sancta Simplicitas" (182), a name which in Goethe's play refers to more than just divine simplicity, but which in Alcott's novel aptly describes Gladys's more modest virtues. Helwyze has decorated his home in "dusky splendour" (101), much like the red splendors that Mephisto shows Faust, the dominant color reminding one of hellfire.

But Alcott is not simply rewriting Goethe; the title of the book is *A Modern Mephistophiles,* and it is the modernity that makes significant differences. One of the most original parts of Goethe's conception of the Faust story is the Gretchen episodes, which are without precedent in the history of the legend. The story of the young girl seduced and then left to deal with the ignominy of pregnancy, the decision to kill her baby and her consequent madness, and the final execution as an infanticide are the concerns of eighteenth-century domestic drama. In her modernization Alcott makes "woman's influence" the focus of the story. Gladys is not degraded by her love for Canaris, nor is her child illegitimate. She is described as "pale, cold innocence" (46) rather than in the sexual, sensual terms that fit Gretchen; in fact, Gladys's sexuality is no lure to Canaris and becomes apparent only in her uninhibited theatricals under the influence of hashish. In her modernization of the story Alcott frames it in much more socially acceptable terms by keeping both Gladys and Olivia free of the stigma of illicit love. She also does not use the magical, visionary, surreal devices that Goethe's Mephistophiles has at his command. The most uncannily satanic aspects of Helwyze's power are his ability to hypnotize, using what was called "animal magnetism" at the time, and his use of hashish on the unsuspecting Gladys. The bond he makes with Canaris is neither diabolical nor actually illegal.

By defusing the story of its magnificent malevolence and supernatural device, Alcott thereby focuses on the "Woman-Soul," what she saw as the real power of women to guide and save men. But as the keeper of men's souls, a woman had an obligation to keep her own soul pure and above reproach, as Gladys does; her shining example touches everyone around her, even Helwyze; and though she is not successful in saving him, she does "influence" Olivia and Canaris to turn away from Helwyze's more diabolical schemes.

The book also points to the power of mothers as well as wives to influence men. Gladys wears a cross, a piece of jewelry left to her by her mother, to remind her of her faith; in hearing the story of it, Felix is reminded of his own mother, and thereupon resolves to marry Gladys even though he does not love her, if only to do what he can to protect her from Helwyze. In her pregnancy Gladys hangs a picture of the Annunciation above her chair and is compared to the ultimate mother in Christian tradition, the Virgin Mary. At one point she is called a Madonna. And it is Olivia's recollection of her own child, a girl who dies in infancy, that solidifies her bond with Gladys, since Gladys takes Olivia as her adopted mother, and the two are drawn together by their shared bond of motherhood.

Alcott also modernizes the book by using many of the devices evident in the thrillers, the original inspiration for the story in 1866. The animal magnetism, the taking of hashish, the powerful older man who in the end is cheated out of his spoils by the women, the elegant and magnificent European setting, the emotions that run high among the beautiful, talented, and wealthy, are all devices used in the gothic stories of Alcott's earlier career. But, in a departure from her earlier stores, Gladys the heroine is not a character of action or emotional breadth, as are Jean Muir of "Behind a Mask" or Virginie Varens of "V. V.: or, Plots and Counterplots." Gladys is not capable of evil, and though she may triumph in the end, the victory is undercut by her death and the sentimentality of her angelic departure to heaven. Olivia is more typical of Alcott's gothic heroines, but even she is denied any real effectiveness in the story because her most significant action—saving Canaris from Helwyze—is carried out on Gladys's authority. Yet the reader must be careful not to condemn *A Modern Mephistophiles* for the defusing that Alcott executed on the manuscript between its too-sensational origins as a rejected thriller in 1866 and its acceptable book form for Roberts Brothers in 1877; the idea of woman's influence was intensely interesting to the reading public at the time, and the sentimentality was in perfectly good popular literary taste. Of course, *A Modern Mephistophiles* is not the epic that Goethe's *Faust* or Dante's *Divine Comedy* was, nor was Alcott trying to write about such large heroes or topics—but the book does show her continuing interest in writing gothic stories for adults.

The book is intensely literary, as is Goethe's work, with allusions and direct references to writers and literary characters both modern and classical. Helwyze's library has in it, among other books, Greek tragedy, Goethe's *Faust,* and Gustave Doré's illustrations of Dante's *Divine Comedy.* When Helwyze blackmails Canaris into marrying Gladys (by threatening to seduce and marry her himself, thereby insuring her spiritual destruction), he insists only that he marry her; if the marriage does not work out, Canaris may behave as Byron did and leave her. Helwyze discusses Nathaniel Hawthorne's *The Scarlet Letter* with Gladys and introduces her to books by philosophers, many of whom are atheists, which she suspects are meant to tempt her away from her faith.

The book shows very heavy foreshadowing in plot. The similarity to Goethe's work suggested by the title *A Modern Mephistophiles* is one indication that Gladys will die and Canaris will be saved, the fates of Gretchen and Faust. Beyond that, however, Gladys's suggestion that Canaris not kill off the hero of a metrical romance he is writing (really authored by Helwyze, but Gladys does not know this), but save him and instead kill off his beloved is another indication of how the story will end. Further, when Olivia finds that Gladys is pregnant, she tells her of her own child who died in infancy, a clear hint that Gladys's unborn child will not live.

As a whole, the book reveals Alcott's continuing interest in the gothic as well as the energy she could, when she wanted, muster for writing in the sentimental mode. *A Modern Mephistophiles* is contemporary with *Under the Lilacs,* her least interesting juvenile novel. The contrast, not only in style but also in invention, is striking. Though *A Modern Mephistophiles* is conventional in some respects, especially in the character of Gladys, Alcott was not simply bowing to her public's desire for the usual kinds of characters found in sentimental fiction. She used the conventions of both gothic and sentimental fiction to explore the darker side of human nature, which is revealed only in glimpses in her juvenile novels.

The Children's Author in the Adult Arena

These works for adults span the entirety of Alcott's writing career and mirror her development as a writer. This development is especially clear in her revision of *Moods:* in the 1864 edition she followed her editor's advice rather than her own instincts as a writer; those instincts were much keener in her later career when she not only restored some parts cut from the first edition, but also considerably rewrote the novel to concentrate attention more on her heroine.

In these works Alcott deals with the realistic problems of adult life, specifically those of working women and those of the relations between men and women in a world which clearly differentiated the roles of the sexes. Though she never clearly resolves the issues involved in love and marriage, she does at least broach the idea of the workable marriage in *Work* and in the revision of *Moods*. Likewise, Alcott deals with the issues of good and evil in her gothic works, although in a less realistic, more emotionally evocative manner. She explores the depths of human depravity as well as the heights of the human capacity for beauty, truth, and goodness. She never dealt at such length with either the psychological depths or the emotional liabilities of human beings in her children's books, but she was not therefore incapable of doing so. In her works for both children and adults she made compromises with literary conventions, sheltering children and even occasionally pandering to adult popular literary tastes. But Alcott was aware of these compromises. She dealt with them as honestly as she could, bending to public taste and yet not compromising her art: her characters may take conventional paths, but they try them in unconventional ways, as Sylvia Yule and Christie Devon demonstrate.

Chapter Five
Influence and Tradition

Louisa May Alcott stands as one of the great American practitioners of the girls' novel and the family story. Her novels for children show her originality, especially when compared to other novels for children in her time. Alcott's child heroes and heroines are always flawed; though the faults of Rose Campbell and Polly Milton may be simply added on to their otherwise excellent characters, Jo March's temper and Dan Kean's violence are integral parts of their characters which are improved upon only by protracted struggle. It is their willingness to struggle with their faults, and the persistence of these faults in spite of all efforts to correct them that make Alcott's most successful stories survive. These novels endure and are read by children today because of the vitality of her characters, both male and female, as well as her honesty in dealing with both their admirable and less commendable traits. The most successful elements of the better children's books are absent in the less satisfactory ones: the presentation of believable characters in situations that try their moral fiber, the sense of humor and fun that the characters exhibit when faced with the injustices of the world, and the rich specificity of the comfortable yet simple lives she presents.

Alcott may be best known for her juvenile novels, but her works for adults are remarkably good, again for the same reasons that her children's novels succeed: skill in building character and then an equal skill in letting the character act out his or her fate, however unpopular or unusual the course of action might be. Alcott composed in a number of adult modes, including poetry and drama. Her most noteworthy adult novel, the 1881 revision of *Moods,* shows her evenhanded skill in dialogue and character development, as well as her sense of propriety about the more exotic style which existed in uncomfortable tandem with the novel of sentiment in the earlier version of the book. The revised novel focuses much more clearly on Sylvia and the problems of her character than it did in its earlier form, and the later ending shows a more realistic, less sentimental sense of life than did the earlier. Alcott confined the melodramatic aspect of her talent to her gothic short stories and her sensational novel *A Modern Mephistophiles,* where it more properly belonged and where the more lurid aspects of her imagination could have free play. In these gothic stories she shows her capacity for embodying malevolence. Though nothing so terrible happens in any of her children's novels, it is not because Alcott was incapable or unwilling to face the darker side of human nature; rather, she kept to the lighter side which was more appropriate to her children's novels, only hinting at the darker which she explored in greater detail in her more dramatic adult works. She maintained this duality in her writing not only because she did not wish to endanger her reputation as a writer for children and thereby diminish her royalties, but also because she was mindful of the proprieties of writing for either audience. Again, though she paid attention to these proprieties, she was not utterly ruled by them; in her best works, *Little Women* and *Little Men,* her unconventionality comes through, enriching the genre in which she wrote while conforming to its dictates. This creative tension adds interest to those of her works that have previously been criticized for their utter conventionality.

In her novels one of the most important themes is the salubrious effect of honest labor. Whether one is rich, like Rose Campbell, who makes philanthropy her profession, or poor, like Christie Devon, who finds that though she is willing to work, not all work is healthy, nor does honest work always pay enough for her to live decently, every character finds a vocation. For the women, the vocation is frequently marriage and motherhood, the traditional happy ending of comedy and domestic fiction. Though some of the married women have other work outside the home—Mrs. March her social work, Jo March Bhaer her teaching and writing, Christine Devon Sterling her florist shop and political organizing—the emphasis in each woman's life is her power in the home. From an early age, Alcott's young girls, both characters and readers, are taught about the "influence" that a wife and mother has inside her home. She can be a force for moral good, social respectability, and love of aesthetic beauty by enticing the members of her household to follow her examples and to take her good advice. Alcott heroines may be unusual in their pursuit of careers outside the home; the most notable example is Nan Harding, who becomes a doctor and remains a spinster. But even these women have their spheres of "influence," acting in the world as examples to other women and as forces of healing and improvement for men.

In her adult works Alcott was more adventurous in investigating the difficulties that the sentimental novels for children ignored. The social issues which may be lightly touched on in the juveniles are explored in greater depth in the adult works. For instance, in *Moods* she does not simply present the platitude of the happy marriage and its resulting domestic harmony. Rather, she explores the difficulties of mismatched married couples and even suggests, although the heroine does not pursue, the avenue of divorce. Human beings as Alcott imagined them were perfectly capable of mistreating each other and of doing so without remorse or any desire to reform, as is clear from her gothic short stories, although in these stories Alcott is not interested in the larger philosophical or social issues; in these works it is usually generalized evil, rather than a specific social ill, that triumphs and even flourishes, even in the face of social snobbery and criminality.

But in her realistic fiction, both for adults and children, Alcott investigated social problems in some depth. Her characters may work, but they have particular difficulties in finding labor that pays enough, as well as in finding entrances into their chosen professions because of the social snobbery that hard, honest work may bring them. Polly Milton is barred from fashionable society because she is a music teacher. Nat Blake is a poor but good boy, and can marry Daisy Brooke only after he proves his worthiness. Though social barriers are a fact of life, Alcott characters survive and conquer them, rather than succumb to them. This is especially true of the feminist issues that Alcott presents, women's suffrage and education especially. Characters such as Josie Brooke, Jo March Bhaer, Rose Campbell, and Christie Devon all have feminist ideas and act upon them with difficulty but also with success in Alcott's fiction.

Alcott's view of women's education, another of her themes, is particularly advanced for the time, for she advocated sensible and practical—rather than fashionable—dress, and practical education as preparation for life rather than the stylish lessons available at finishing schools. She thought that all girls, even rich ones like Rose Campbell, should be prepared for womanhood by learning housework, including cooking and sewing. According to Alcott, boys and girls alike should be taught about the world they will live in by experiencing it, rather than by memorizing and reading from textbooks in classrooms. Corporal punishment was absolutely out of the question; instead, parents and teachers should rule by love and moral suasion. Though most of these ideas are acceptable now, they were advanced for Alcott's time; many were borrowed from her father, Bronson Alcott. Even in those children's novels that are not primarily concerned with education, the theme is an isssue.

Recent Alcott criticism, especially that comparing her writing for adults and that for children, has judged the children's novels inadequate, either because of the sentimentality of the situations and characters or because of what is perceived as Alcott's failure to face up to her own life in her more autobiographical novels. The sentimentality of the literature of Alcott's time must be taken into account; it was so pervasive because readers found it interesting. The plight of a woman confined by social status, sexual prejudice, defect in character, or poverty in spite of her obvious worth was a popular theme; Alcott protagonists overcome their limitations by hard work and faith in God. Becoming a wife, mother, and good Christian at the end of a novel shows not so much a character capitulating to literary stereotype but more the power of that character to overcome seemingly impossible barriers to such earthly happiness and success. Furthermore, Alcott heroines do not always choose the most likely marriage partners nor the traditional "happily ever after" fates of more conventional heroines. In their married lives they pursue active careers and social change. Alcott in her more successful novels rarely chooses to tie up the ends of her narrative in a neat, predictable bow, though she does not go as far as she did in her own life, which was so unconventional that it hardly made acceptable fiction without sweeping revision. The atypical characters she creates continue to be iconoclasts even, ironically, when they are likely to become ordinary stock figures in their conventional adult lives. Therein lies the strength of her most enduring characters, especially Jo March.

Alcott's works for children have endured in spite of adverse scholarly criticism and changing literary tastes. Compared with children's literature of our own times, Alcott's books are "safe," without the modern problems that occur frequently in today's children's novels—sexuality, drug abuse, divorce, and the like. This lack of controversy may account for some of the popularity; the longevity is also due to the nostalgia with which adults remember Alcott's books and the fervor with which they recommend them to succeeding generations of children, especially girls. These girls, in their turn, find *Little Women* so enjoyable that they read all the other Alcott juveniles they can find. This mentality for reading all books in a series is cultivated by publishers, who bring out uniform editions, not only of Alcott's works, but works by others as well. Though the best of the books show Alcott's artistic complexity, even the least satisfactory of them is enjoyable. The greater sophistication of older readers also finds play in her novels, both for the adult who returns to them after a considerable time, and for the scholar, who is most likely to judge the literary sophistication in greatest depth.

But children and nostalgic adults do not have infallible taste in literature; certainly some of Alcott's juveniles have survived for the same reason that they sold when originally published: simply because Alcott, the author whose name was already established, wrote them. Alcott knew which scenes and themes were important to her novels' financial success, and so she repeated them in later books, with some slight variation. For many female readers the gratification of the conventional happy ending, replete with marriage to an attractive man, is satisfying; it is a tribute to Alcott's literary ingenuity that she could say anything new in the several novels where her readers demanded, and still demand, such a stereotypical ending as the only satisfying one possible.

But even where she would most likely slip into cliché, Alcott's skill convinced and still convinces her readers that the optimism, warmth, and affection with which she portrayed her characters were sincere. These ideals remain, in spite of the clichés which have surrounded them, important values to children and adults and account for the popularity of her books not only in this country but also around the world. The home is pictured as such an accepting, loving place that even the most jaded reader may be seduced into believing the simple exterior that Alcott books present. The many material pleasures, however small, that the characters enjoy, if only vicariously at times, are so realistically and vividly presented that readers find the exterior convincing and inviting and therefore relinquish suspicions about Alcott's other messages of spirituality and self-sacrifice, much as such a reader might otherwise mistrust them. No doubt, because of the age of the books, some of the interest in them by young readers is historical curiosity—how did young people live, dress, eat, in the nineteenth century? But the themes of happy family life, honest, hard work that eventually overcomes realistically portrayed difficulties, and eventually growing up, marrying, and having a family of one's own have enduring significance. Even modern readers believe in such values, though they have been much mistreated and sentimentalized elsewhere.

Notes and References

Chapter Two

1. Madeleine B. Stern, "The First Appearance of a 'Little Women' Incident," *American Notes and Queries* 3 (October 1943):99–100.
2. Nina Auerbach, "Austen and Alcott on Matriarchy: New Women or New Wives?", *Novel* 10 (Fall 1976):18.
3. Frank Preston Stearns, *Sketches from Concord and Appledore: Concord Thirty Years Ago. . .* (New York: Putnam, 1895), p. 83.
4. *Little Women: or Meg, Jo, Beth, and Amy* (1868–69; reprinted, Boston and Toronto, 1915), p. 381; hereafter page references cited in parentheses in the text.
5. Cited by Cornelia Meigs in preface, Lucile Gulliver, comp., *Louisa May Alcott: a Bibliography* (Boston, 1932), pp. 22, 29.
6. Harriet Beecher Stowe, *Uncle Tom's Cabin: Or, Life Among the Lowly* (1852; reprint ed., Boston and New York: Houghton Mifflin, 1896), 2:52.
7. Cited in Gulliver, *Bibliography*, p. 29.
8. Auerbach, "Austen and Alcott," p. 17.
9. Ibid., pp. 17–20.
10. Ibid., p. 21.
11. Martha Saxton, *Louisa May: A Modern Biography of Louisa May Alcott* (Boston, 1977), pp. 9, 15.
12. Brigid Brophy, "Sentimentality and Louisa M. Alcott; A Masterpiece and Dreadful," *New York Times Book Review,* January 17, 1975, pp. 1, 44.
13. *Little Men* (1871; reprint ed., Boston and Toronto, 1913), p. 21; hereafter page references cited in parentheses in the text.
14. I am grateful to William Blackburn and his unpublished paper "The Intentional Fallacies of Louisa May Alcott" for pointing out many of these peculiar features in *Little Men.*
15. *Jo's Boys And How They Turned Out: A Sequel to Little Men* (1886; reprint ed., Boston and Toronto, 1953), pp. 1–2; hereafter page references cited in the text are to this 1953 edition, *except* as otherwise noted.

Chapter Three

1. Saxton, *Louisa May;* p. 303.
2. *An Old-Fashioned Girl* (1870; reprint ed., Boston and Toronto, 1911), p. 10; hereafter page references cited in parentheses in the text.

3. Madeleine B. Stern, *Louisa May Alcott* (Norman, OK, 1950), p. 192.

4. *Eight Cousins: Or, The Aunt Hill* (1875; reprint ed., Boston and Toronto, 1927), p. 40; hereafter page references cited in parentheses in the text.

5. *Rose in Bloom: A Sequel to "Eight Cousins"* (1876; reprint ed., Boston and Toronto, 1927), p. 37; hereafter page references cited in parentheses in the text.

6. Ann Douglas, *The Feminization of American Culture* (New York: Avon, 1977), pp. 51–55.

7. *Under the Lilacs* (1878; reprint ed., Boston and Toronto, 1927), p. 32; hereafter page references cited in parentheses in the text.

8. *Jack and Jill* (1880; reprint ed., Boston and Toronto, 1928), p. 9; hereafter page references cited in parentheses in the text.

Chapter Four

1. *Hospital Sketches* (Boston, 1863), p. 10; hereafter page references cited in parentheses in the text.

2. *Moods: A Novel,* rev. ed. (Boston, 1881), preface. All other quotations are taken from the novel's first edition (Boston, 1864); hereafter page references cited in parentheses in the text.

3. Saxton, *Louisa May,* p. 277.

4. Leona Rostenberg, "Some Anonymous and Pseudonymous Thrillers of Louisa M. Alcott," *Bibliographical Society of America Papers* 37 (1943): 131–40.

5. Madeleine B. Stern, ed. *Behind a Mask: The Unknown Thrillers of Louisa May Alcott* (New York, 1975), p. xix.

6. *Work: A Story of Experience* (Boston, 1973), p. 266; hereafter page references cited in parentheses in the text.

7. Saxton, *Louisa May,* p. 320.

8. *A Modern Mephistophiles,* No Name Series (Boston, 1877), p. 290; hereafter page references cited in parentheses in the text.

Selected Bibliography

PRIMARY SOURCES

1. Novels and Books

Eight Cousins: Or, The Aunt Hill. Boston: Roberts Brothers, 1875. Reprint. Orchard House Edition. Boston and Toronto: Little, Brown, 1927.

Hospital Sketches. Boston: James Redpath, 1863. Reprint with introduction by Earl Schenck Miers. American Century Series. New York:. Sagamore Press, 1957.

Jack and Jill: A Village Story. Boston: Roberts Brothers, 1880. Reprint. Orchard House Edition. Boston and Toronto: Little, Brown, 1928.

Jo's Boys And How They Turned Out: A Sequel to Little Men. Boston: Roberts Brothers, 1886. Reprint. Orchard House Edition. Boston and Toronto: Little, Brown, 1953.

Little Men: Life at Plumfield with Jo's Boys. Boston: Roberts Brothers, 1873. Reprint. Orchard House Edition. Boston and Toronto: Little, Brown, 1913.

Little Women: or Meg, Jo, Beth, and Amy. Boston: Roberts Brothers, 1868–69. 2 vols. Reprint. Orchard House Edition. Boston and Toronto: Little, Brown, 1915.

A Modern Mephistophiles. No Name Series. Boston: Roberts Brothers, 1877.

Moods. Boston:. A. K. Loring, 1864. Revised ed. *Moods: A Novel.* Boston: Roberts Brothers, 1881.

An Old-Fashioned Girl. Boston: Roberts Brothers, 1870. Reprint. Orchard House Edition. Boston and Toronto: Little, Brown, 1911.

Rose in Bloom: A Sequel to "Eight Cousins." Boston: Roberts Brothers, 1876. Reprint. Orchard House Edition. Boston and Toronto: Little, Brown, 1927.

Under the Lilacs. Boston: Roberts Brothers, 1877. Reprint. Orchard House Edition. Boston and Toronto: Little, Brown, 1927.

Work: A Story of Experience. Boston: Roberts Brothers, 1873. Reprint with introduction by Elizabeth Hardwick. New York: Arno, 1977.

2. Short Story Collections
Aunt Jo's Scrap Bag Series
>   *My Boys.* Boston: Roberts Brothers, 1872.
>   *Shawl Straps.* Boston: Roberts Brothers, 1872.
>   *Cupid and Chow-Chow.* Boston: Roberts Brothers, 1874.
>   *My Girls.* Boston: Roberts Brothers, 1878.
>   *Jimmy's Cruise in the Pinafore.* Boston: Roberts Brothers, 1879.
>   *An Old-Fashioned Thanksgiving.* Boston: Roberts Brothers, 1882.
Behind a Mask: The Unknown Thrillers of Louisa May Alcott. Edited with intro-
>   duction by Madeleine B. Stern. New York: William Morrow, 1975.
Flower Fables. Boston: George W. Briggs, 1854. Reprint. Children's Literature
>   Reprint Series. Great Neck, N.Y.: Core Collections, 1977.
A Garland for Girls. Boston: Roberts Brothers, 1888. Reprint. New York:
>   Grosset and Dunlap, 1908.
*Glimpses of Louisa: A Centennial Sampling of the Best Short Stories by Louisa May
>   Alcott.* Edited by Cornelia Meigs. Boston and Toronto: Little, Brown,
>   1968.
Lulu's Library Series
>   *A Christmas Dream.* Boston: Roberts Brothers, 1886.
>   *The Frost King.* Boston: Roberts Brothers, 1887.
>   *Recollections.* Boston: Roberts Brothers, 1889.
Morning-Glories, and Other Stories. New York: Carlton, 1867.
On Picket Duty, and other Tales. Boston: James Redpath; New York: H. Dexter,
>   Hamilton and Company, 1864. Reprint. American Short Story Series.
>   Vol. 3. New York: Garrett Press, 1969.
Plots and Counterplots: More Unknown Thrillers of Louisa May Alcott. New York:
>   William Morrow, 1976.
Proverb Stories. Boston: Roberts Brothers, 1882.
A Round Dozen: Stories by Louisa May Alcott. Introduction by Anne Thaxter
>   Eaton. New York: Viking, 1963.
Silver Pitchers: and Independence, A Centennial Love Story. Boston: Roberts
>   Brothers, 1876.
Spinning-Wheel Stories. Boston: Roberts Brothers, 1884.

3. Miscellaneous
Comic Tragedies Written by "Jo and Meg" and Acted by the "Little Women." Edited by
>   Anna Alcott Pratt. Boston: Roberts Brothers, 1893.
Diana and Persis. Edited by Sarah Elbert. New York: Arno, 1978.
Will's Wonder Book. The Dirigo Series. Vol. 2. Boston: Horace B. Fuller, 1870.
>   Reprint. Madeleine B. Stern, ed. *Louisa's Wonder Book: An Unknown Alcott
>   Juvenile.* Mount Pleasant: Central Michigan University and Clarke Histor-
>   ical Library, 1975.

SECONDARY SOURCES

1. Bibliographies and biographies

Anthony, Katharine. *Louisa May Alcott.* New York: Knopf, 1938. One of the first psychoanalytic studies of Alcott's life; examines the complex relationships among Alcott family members.

Cheney, Ednah Dow. *Louisa May Alcott: Her Life, Letters, and Journals.* Boston: Roberts Brothers, 1889. An important source for Alcott's private writings, considerably edited in order to present Alcott as a dutiful, helpful daughter and a writer unimpeachably motivated to help her family and to present moral fiction for the young.

Gulliver, Lucile, compiler. *Louisa May Alcott: A Bibliography.* Preface by Cornelia Meigs. Boston: Little, Brown, 1932. An early bibliography of all known editions of Alcott's works at the time; Meigs in the preface praises Alcott for her frankness in her children's novels.

Payne, Alma J. *Louisa May Alcott: A Reference Guide.* Boston: G. K. Hall, 1980. Most comprehensive bibliography of secondary sources on Alcott.

Saxton, Martha. *Louisa May: A Modern Biography of Louisa May Alcott.* Boston: Houghton Mifflin, 1977. A psychoanalytical interpretation of Alcott's life, work, and family relations. The critical commentary on the novels results in an elevation of the adult novels at the expense of the juveniles. Particularly good in presenting the historical milieu in which Alcott lived.

Stern, Madeleine B. *Louisa May Alcott.* Norman: University of Oklahoma Press, 1950; 2d ed. rev., 1971. The definitive critical biography of Alcott, especially important for bibliographic details not elsewhere available; second edition contains the most comprehensive bibliography of Alcott's writings.

————, ed. *Louisa's Wonder Book: An Unknown Alcott Juvenile.* Mount Pleasant: Central Michigan University and Clarke Historical Library, 1975. A reprint of a book published without Alcott's knowledge; also, latest update of Stern's bibliography of Alcott's collected works.

2. Books, articles

Auerbach, Nina. "Austen and Alcott on Matriarchy: New Women or New Wives?" *Novel* 10 (Fall 1976):6–26. Compares *Pride and Prejudice* and *Little Women* as representing matriarchies, but claims that the rich physical detail and warm atmosphere of the March family home undermine the overt message that girls should grow up and become independent of that home.

Baym, Nina. *Woman's Fiction: A Guide to Novels by and about Women in America, 1820–1870.* Ithaca, N.Y. and London: Cornell University Press, 1978, pp. 196–99. Discusses *Little Women* as girls' fiction and as the culmination of the domestic fiction of women earlier in the century.

Brophy, Brigid. "Sentimentality and Louisa M. Alcott: A Masterpiece, and Dreadful." *New York Times Book Review,* January 17, 1975, pp. 1, 44. Discusses Alcott's sentimentality as a way of avoiding full characterization in *Little Women.*

Darling, Richard L. "Authors vs. Critics: Children's Books in the 1870's." *Publishers Weekly,* October 16, 1967, pp. 25–27. A description of the literary rivalry between Alcott and William T. Adams which surfaced in *Eight Cousins.*

Ellis, Kate. "Life with Marmee: Three Versions." In *The Classic American Novel and the Movies,* edited by Gerald Peary and Roger Shatzkin, pp. 62–72. New York: Ungar, 1977. A discussion of the movie versions of *Little Women* in comparison with the novel.

Gay, Carol. "The Philosopher and His Daughter: Amos Bronson Alcott and Louisa." *Essays in Literature* (Western Illinois University), 2 (1975):181–91. Suggests that Alcott's misunderstanding of her father resulted from psychological immaturity throughout her life.

Janeway, Elizabeth. "Meg, Jo, Beth and Amy." *New York Times Book Review,* September 29, 1968, pp. 42–46. Finds that the perennial interest of *Little Women* lies in the character of Jo as a nascent feminist.

Kelly, Robert Gordon. *Mother was a Lady: Self and Society in Selected American Children's Periodicals, 1865–1890.* Westport, Conn.: Greenwood Press, 1974. Numerous references to Alcott's short stories for children in various children's periodicals.

"Recent Literature." *Atlantic Monthly* 40, no. 237 (July, 1877): 109. A favorable review of *A Modern Mephistophiles,* speculating that its author is Julian Hawthorne.

Rostenberg, Leona. "Some Anonymous and Pseudonymous Thrillers of Louisa M. Alcott." *Bibliographical Society of America Papers* 37 (1943):131–40. The first account of Alcott's gothic thrillers, including bibliographic details.

Russ, Lavinia. "Not to be Read on Sunday." *Horn Book* 44 (1968):521–26. A centennial celebration of *Little Women,* praising the book for its presentation of bravery and goodness.

Smith, Grover, Jr. "The Doll-Burners: D. H. Lawrence and Louisa Alcott." *Modern Language Quarterly* 19 (1958):28–32. An interesting contrast between scenes in *Little Men* and *Sons and Lovers,* highlighting a peculiar incident in Alcott's book.

Spacks, Patricia Meyer. *The Female Imagination.* New York: Alfred A. Knopf, 1975, pp. 95–101. Examines *Little Women* and the virtues of self-control that the March sisters are taught, which make them less vigorous characters.

Stern, Madeleine B. "The First Appearance of a 'Little Women' Incident." *American Notes and Queries* 3 (October 1943):99–100. Discusses the appearance of the Christmas breakfast incident in *Merry's Museum.*

————. "Louisa Alcott's Feminist Letters." *Studies in the American Renaissance,* 1978, pp. 429–52. A collection of and commentary on Alcott's letters to various periodicals about the women's movement in her time.

————. "Louisa M. Alcott: An Appraisal." *New England Quarterly* 22 (1949):475–98. Suggests that the fame of *Little Women* stems both from its universality and the particularity with which it portrays New England life.

————. "Louisa M. Alcott's Contributions to Periodicals, 1848–1868." *More Books: The Bulletin of the Boston Public Library* 18 (1943):411–20. Discusses the wide range of Alcott's short stories, both for children and adults, and how this range contributed to her literary skills in writing *Little Women.*

————. "Louisa M. Alcott's Self-Criticism." *More Books: The Bulletin of the Boston Public Library* 20 (1945):339–45. Examines a number of Alcott's short stories about writers and writing and finds articulated there Alcott's predilection for realism and simplicity.

————. "The Witch's Cauldron to the Family Hearth: Louisa M. Alcott's Literary Development, 1848–1868." *More Books: The Bulletin of the Boston Public Library* 18 (1943):363–80. Sketches of Alcott's early career and survey of the sentimental and gothic fiction, and their contribution to her skill as a novelist in *Little Women.*

Strickland, Charles. "A Transcendentalist Father: The Child-Rearing Practices of Bronson Alcott." *History of Childhood Quarterly* 1 (1973):4–51. Discusses the journals that Bronson Alcott kept on the growth of Anna and Louisa Alcott and the repression that resulted from his peculiar theories of child nurture.

Vincent, Elizabeth. "Subversive Miss Alcott." *New Republic* 40, no. 204 (October 22, 1924):204. Attributes *Little Women's* popularity to children's continuing desire for clearly portrayed morality.

Index

110

LOUISA MAY ALCOTT

fiction and autobiography, *see* autobiography and fiction
Flag of Our Union, The, 82, 88
Frank Leslie's Illustrated Newspaper, 82
Fredericksburg, Battle of, 5, 73
Fruitlands, 2–3

girls' education, 7, 70, 97; in *Eight Cousins,* 51–54; in *Jack and Jill,* 67–68; in *Jo's Boys,* 42–43; in *Little Men,* 33–34; in *An Old-Fashioned Girl,* 45–46
Goethe, *Faust,* 7, 89–91
gothic, in *A Modern Mephistophiles,* 92; *see also* short stories, gothic

hashish, in *A Modern Mephistophiles,* 89–92
Hawthorne, *Scarlet Letter, The,* 80, 93
Hughes, Thomas, *Tom Brown's Schooldays,* 15, 31

Lawrence, Rhoda, 8–9
Lee and Shepard, publishers, 12, 55
local color, 12, 65, 69
longevity, of Alcott's works, 95; of *Little Women,* 98; of March family stories, 10
Loring, A. K., publisher, 75

March, Beth, 13; death, 14, 16–17, 22–23, 26; modelled after Elizabeth Alcott, 4
March, Jo, 7, 13; in *Jo's Boys,* 37; in *Little Men,* 35–36; marriage, 23, 26–27; relationship with Amy March, 28; sons of, 23; temper of, 21–22; writing, 24, 26, 43
marriage, 96; in adult novels, 94; in *Eight Cousins,* 60–62; in *Good Wives,* 14–15; in *Jo's Boys,* 41–43; in *Little Women,* 14, 18, 22–27; in

March family stories, 11; in *A Modern Mephistophiles,* 89; in *Moods,* 76–81, 97; in *An Old-Fashioned Girl,* 48–50; in *Rose in Bloom,* 59–62; in *Under the Lilacs,* 64; in *Work,* 85, 87–88; *see also* divorce
medicine, Alcott's nursing experience, 5–6; as woman's career, 33–34, 38; in *Eight Cousins,* 54; in *Hospital Sketches,* 73; in *Rose in Bloom,* 61
Merry's Museum, 6, 12–13
motherhood, in *Little Women,* 14, 26–28; in *A Modern Mephistophiles,* 92; in *An Old-Fashioned Girl,* 46

Nieriker, Louisa May, 8
Niles, Thomas, publisher, 6–7, 12–13, 75, 88; as Mr. Tiber in *Jo's Boys,* 38
No Name series, 7, 83, 88
nursing, in *Hospital Sketches,* 73–75; *see also* medicine

Optic, Oliver, 12, 55
originality in Alcott's fiction, *see* conventionality
Otis, James, *Toby Tyler, or Ten Weeks with a Circus,* 63

Peabody, Elizabeth Palmer, 1–2
philanthropy, Alcott family attitude toward, 4, 7; in *An Old-Fashioned Girl,* 47–48; in *Rose in Bloom,* 58–59
physical education, in *Eight Cousins,* 53; in *Jack and Jill,* 67, 69; in *Little Men,* 31–32
play, in *Jack and Jill,* 65, 69; in *Under the Lilacs,* 63
plotting, 43; in *Eight Cousins,* 50–51; in *Jack and Jill,* 65–69; in *Jo's Boys,* 38–39; in *Little Men,* 29; in *Little*